Contents

Acknowledgements

This was the heaviest personal project I've ever lifted and I couldn't have done so without the help of many many people. First, thank you to my family for their encouragement and love, and also furrowed brows of confusion when my ideas made no sense to them, indicating a need for clarification. But mostly the love. Thank you Nora, my biggest supporter in this project and in life. What the HECK would I do without you? You kept reminding me that this was a big project, which I didn't even know I kept needing to hear. You brought life to these scenes and characters. Thank you Arin, for organizing, steering, and fully revising my story. Thank you Hamilton, for cello proofing this thing. Thank you Eric, for your eagle eyes on my woefully not-so-final sheet music draft. Lets just say I'm glad you didn't charge per found mistake... Thank you to Kelly who made a killer cover. Thank you Jenn for your sagely mix advice on the play-alongs. Thank you to my friends, who acted as "beta testers", for your ideas and suggestions. Thank you to all my fellow nerds who encouraged me to be me. This book is for my family.

DRAGONSCALES

The Hero Levels

25 Fantasy Etudes to Slay Evil

Includes audio play-alongs

Nick Revel

VIOLIN

Book design, Kelly Rupert

Story editor, Arin Murphy-Hiscock

Story editor, Nora Krohn

Cello edition proofreader, Hamilton Berry

Engraving proofreader, Eric Allen

Bass performance, Stephen Sas

Art, Nick Revel and Gencraft

Composition, engraving, performing, mixing, layout, videos, Nick Revel

ISBN 979-8-9875124-0-1

© 2024 Nick Revel

All Rights Reserved. International copyright secured.

Foreword

I got back home from a concert in New York City at about 11:00pm the night before our 14-day vacation to Ecuador in June 2023 and said to Nora "I think I'm getting sick." She looked at me and said "No, you can't get sick." And I looked at her and said "I know, but still..." Several hours later I woke up delirious and feverish, aching all over, and somehow cold. The thermometer read 101.9°F. Maybe it'll go away by morning? Not even close. Packing for the trip was so difficult that I nearly fell back asleep and called it all off. But by the time my triple strength ibuprofen horse pill kicked in and I had a negative COVID test in hand, I found myself donning the face mask once again as we boarded an Uber that smelled of those old-fashioned hang-y car fresheners, headed for JFK.

Ecuador was stunningly beautiful, especially driving on roads meandering precariously on nearly vertical mountainsides. However, the route we planned climbed higher and higher into the elevation, into the volcanoes. The bug that was trying to kill me ebbed and flowed but never fully died. It was once we arrived in the remote Chimborazo Lodge, minimal and naturalistic, at 13,123 vertical feet, that my virus and all its replicas reared their ugly heads. I was exhausted, in pain, and could barely eat. Our space heater tried so hard, but I still wore all of my warmest layers under the covers. It was then for the first time that I felt incredibly frustrated and guilty that I was ruining what would have been a perfect trip for Nora. I told her to go out and hike and enjoy. After much persuasion and assurance of my not dying, she reluctantly accepted adventuring in the lunar landscape of Chimborazo.

You might be wondering why I'm saying all of this. Well, here it is: alone with the Alpacas peering into our wood cabin through the window, bored out of my mind, and delirious in my fever dreams, on a whim I drafted the entire *Hero Levels* project from start to finish. Months before, after I had published my first set of books, *DragonScales 3-Octave Scales and Arpeggios,* I said I would never make another book ever again. EVER. But there, after several hours, I had already sketched the skeleton on my phone, setting the ball rolling. The idea to combine a fantasy story, inspired by my childhood nostalgia for role playing games and Japanese anime, with etudes and audio backing tracks that function as the story's soundtrack lit up in my mind like a beacon. "It will be like a video game," I thought.

The plot, the characters, the twists, and the 25 etudes that could match with the various scenes in the story flowed like pure volcano water...or whatever. In my hit list I included improvisation and extended techniques with a real emphasis on creative music making. I reflected on how awful Mazas, Kreutzer, Campagnoli, Dont, and all the others, accompanied by Dr. Beat blasting "ONE TWO THREE FOUR" was for my hormone-addled adolescent brain. Sorry, not sorry. They weren't fun.

Learning the craft of an instrument should be fun! Fun stimulates brain activity and learning happens quicker and more deeply. Why not go on an adventure while learning your instrument? This is what I was thinking high up in my fever in Chimborazo. I wanted to create a large-scale flexible learning tool for multiple instruments and difficulty levels that access multiple sources of creativity along the way. My hope is that you, the player, and the Hero, will play this game and feel inspired to make *your* story come to life. Are you ready, Player?

PLAYER START HERE

Scan the QR code with your smartphone or tablet

Audio Play-Alongs

Practice Tempos

Demo Play-Throughs

Community Space

Chapter One
The Adventure Begins

The Hero from Amberglade

Amberglade, a peaceful village cradled amid rolling hills and ancient woods, has been your haven since infancy. The tragic loss of your parents at the tender age of three has left you with only hazy memories of them, their faces softened by time. Rowena, the steadfast caregiver whom you call aunt, provides you with solace and family, as do your fellow orphans, siblings by circumstance who depend on you, the eldest of the bunch. With a heart that knows only kindness and the will to make the world a better place, you have carved out your place as their guardian, a beacon of hope... or maybe even a hero.

1. The Hero from Amberglade

Nick Revel

Player Start

Welcome to the 1st level, Hero! To find the accompanying audio play-along recordings, scan the QR code on the QR code page. Earbuds, headphones, or quality speakers are recommended.

Variations

Below are optional rhythmic variations for the Hero's theme, to start at bar 3

Below are optional bowing variations for the second theme, to start at bar 19

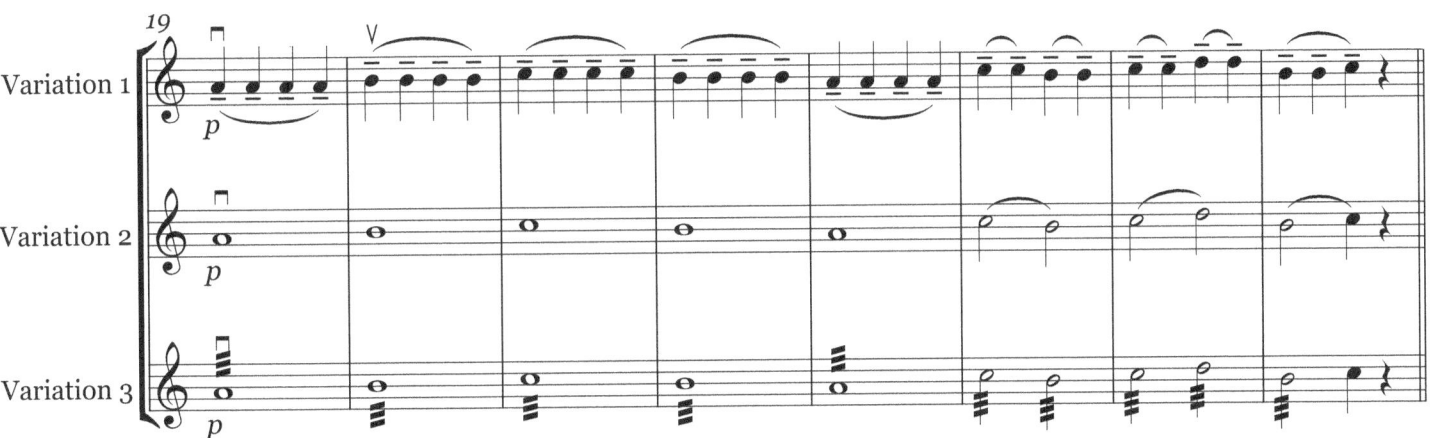

Eldervale Wilds

When whispers of a cursed monster guarding a hidden treasure in the Eldervale Wilds reach your ears, curiosity ignites your adventurous soul. The allure of this treasure beckons: you covet it not only as proof of your worthiness, but also as a means to provide for the beloved orphanage that has raised you. And let there be no doubt: you will succeed. Monsters are mere fairytales, after all; whatever has been seen near the treasure can't be more than an animal. Brimming with zeal, you equip yourself with a rusty sword, a rugged bandana, sturdy trousers, and provisions for your journey, and set forth.

The serene forest beyond Amberglade, with its caressing breeze and musk of untamed nature, lures you further and further from the only home you've ever known. The terrain slowly evolves, taking on new colors and contours as you venture deeper into the woods.

Suddenly, your idyllic excursion takes a treacherous turn. With a ghastly buzzing and the rustling of foliage, a swarm of giant insects emerges from the darkness of the forest, their gargantuan size elevating them from a mere nuisance to life-threatening adversaries. You begin to run, squashing the smallest among them underfoot, but with your every stride, their numbers swell, monstrous both in size and menace.

Desperation drives you further onward in an attempt to escape them, adrenaline surging as the relentless swarm closes in. Blind fear eventually leads you into an outcropping of rock. Looking over your shoulder to gauge the distance of the hideous swarm close at your heels, you miss your footing and find yourself falling, not to the ground, but through a crevasse into darkness. Scrabbling uselessly for something to grab onto, you fall down, down into the dark.

2. Eldervale Wilds

Nick Revel

Just a normal walk in the woods...

Your fun forest adventure turns dangerous when giant bugs attack you! Can you defend yourself by stomping at the right times? Can you make beautiful sounds with your bow when it's safe?

rhythm here is tricky here. do your best!

The track squish timings will sound slightly different than what is notated going forward

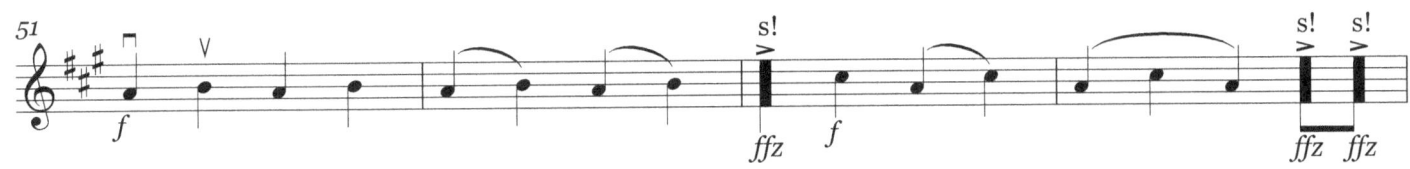

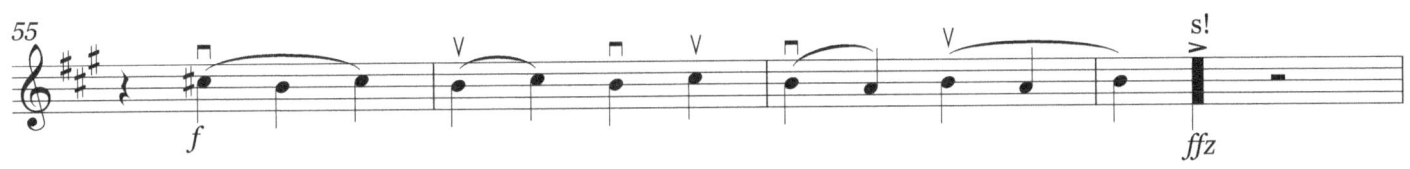

Faster and faster like a bouncy ball

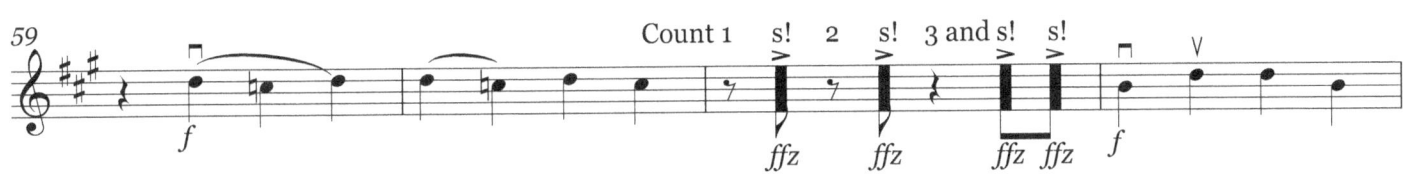

Monsters Are Real

When your mind clears, fragmented memories of the fall flit through your consciousness. Your entire body throbs, blood trickling from various wounds across your arms and legs. You look around: the rough rock walls and pinprick of daylight straight above you suggest you have fallen into a deep cavern. Feeble torchlight casts eerie, wavering shadows over its jagged expanse. As you contemplate the nature of this underground realm in bewilderment, a silhouette emerges from the obscurity of the cavern's depths.

Initially, relief washes over you at the sight of another presence; perhaps they will aid you in extricating yourself from this dire predicament. But wait; has this mysterious figure tumbled into this forsaken abyss, too? Is it friend, or foe? Questions swirl, and your anxiety deepens as the figure draws nearer.

A disquieting aura surrounds the approaching entity, still cloaked in shadow. Its looming advance rouses the hairs along the nape of your neck, your senses alerted to an impending threat. Your mouth burns with the acrid tang of fear, numbing any residual pain you might have felt from the fall. With each step, the grotesque visage of the figure becomes clearer—an abominable countenance, etched with scars where eyes should be, voids that seem to absorb the feeble light.

With a fresh wave of horror, panic urges you to your feet, the pounding of your heart a frenetic drumbeat echoing in your ears. And you grasp the gruesome truth: either this is only a surreal nightmare, or you are face to face with a genuine monster.

The cacophony of your heartbeat seems all the louder in the cavern's oppressive silence, and your body trembles uncontrollably. With bated breath, you consider your options. Escape, or stand and confront this nightmarish foe? All at once, a wellspring of determination surges from deep inside you, flowing from the deep-rooted resolve to seize the treasure that might lift your orphanage siblings from the clutches of poverty.

An erratic interplay ensues: surfing waves of adrenaline, you sprint past the monster's clutches and rush back into the cover of darkness, trembling and hiding. With every opportunity you swing your rusted sword, a desperate dance to evade the monster's lethal strikes.

3. Monsters are Real

From adventure to horror...

Nick Revel

You've fallen into a dark and scary cave! And, is that a monster?! This etude explores improvisation. How can you create creepy scary sounds by making the material in the boxed "cells" your own?

The Audio Play-Along alternates between the A section, which has no meter or tempo, and the B section, which has a strict tempo of quarter=180. The full form is ABABAB. Choose from the four patterns below to play in each A section. Use your ears to learn when the track switches between sections.

A Section (free time, no tempo)

Trembling in Fear

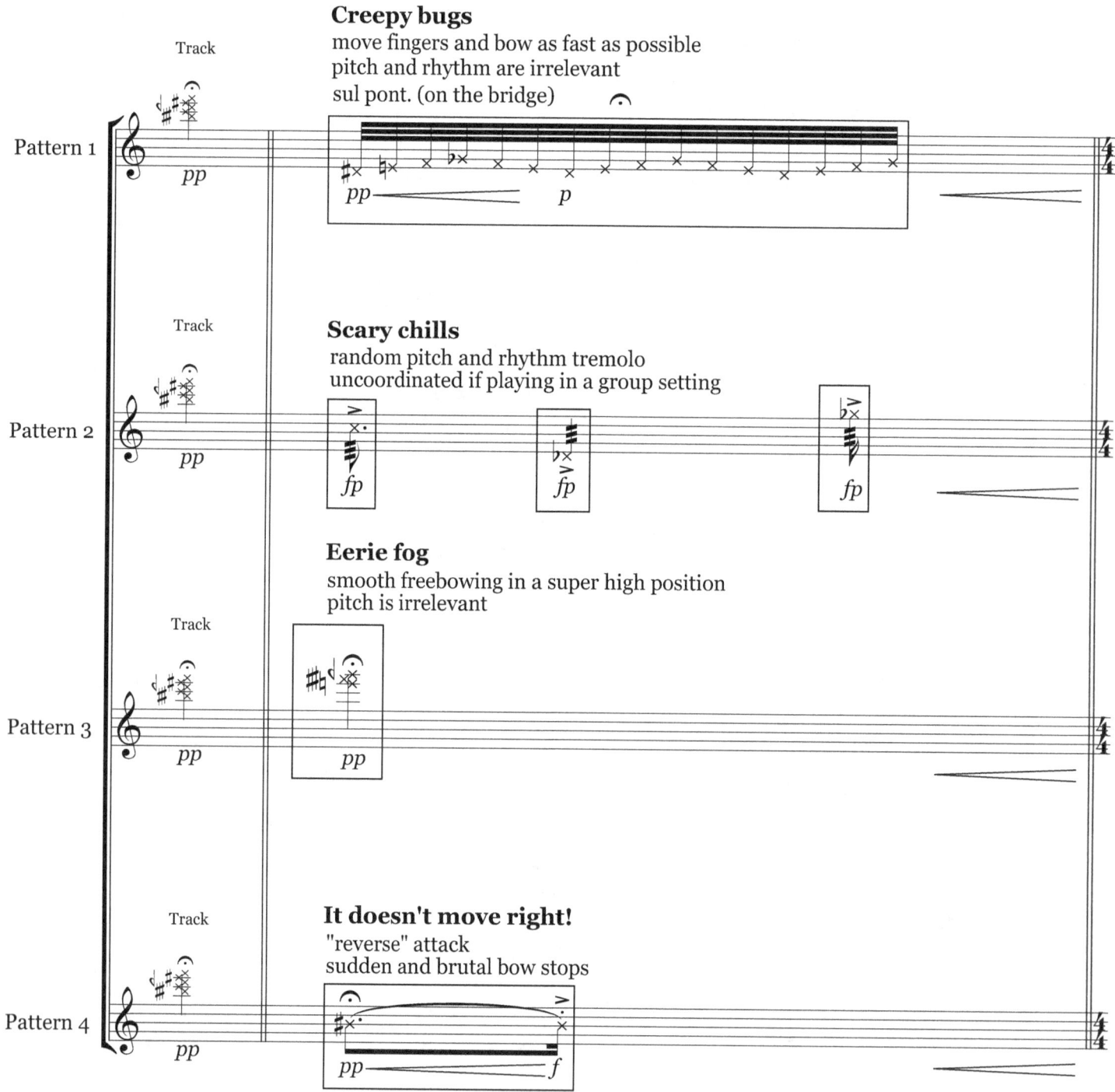

Creepy bugs
move fingers and bow as fast as possible
pitch and rhythm are irrelevant
sul pont. (on the bridge)

Scary chills
random pitch and rhythm tremolo
uncoordinated if playing in a group setting

Eerie fog
smooth freebowing in a super high position
pitch is irrelevant

It doesn't move right!
"reverse" attack
sudden and brutal bow stops

Choose from the four patterns below to play in each B section. To help with finding the tempo, listen for the high metallic drum sound (hi-hat) playing eighth notes in the first B Section. Each B section is a different lengght!

B Section (strict tempo)
Running and fighting for your life

♩ = 180

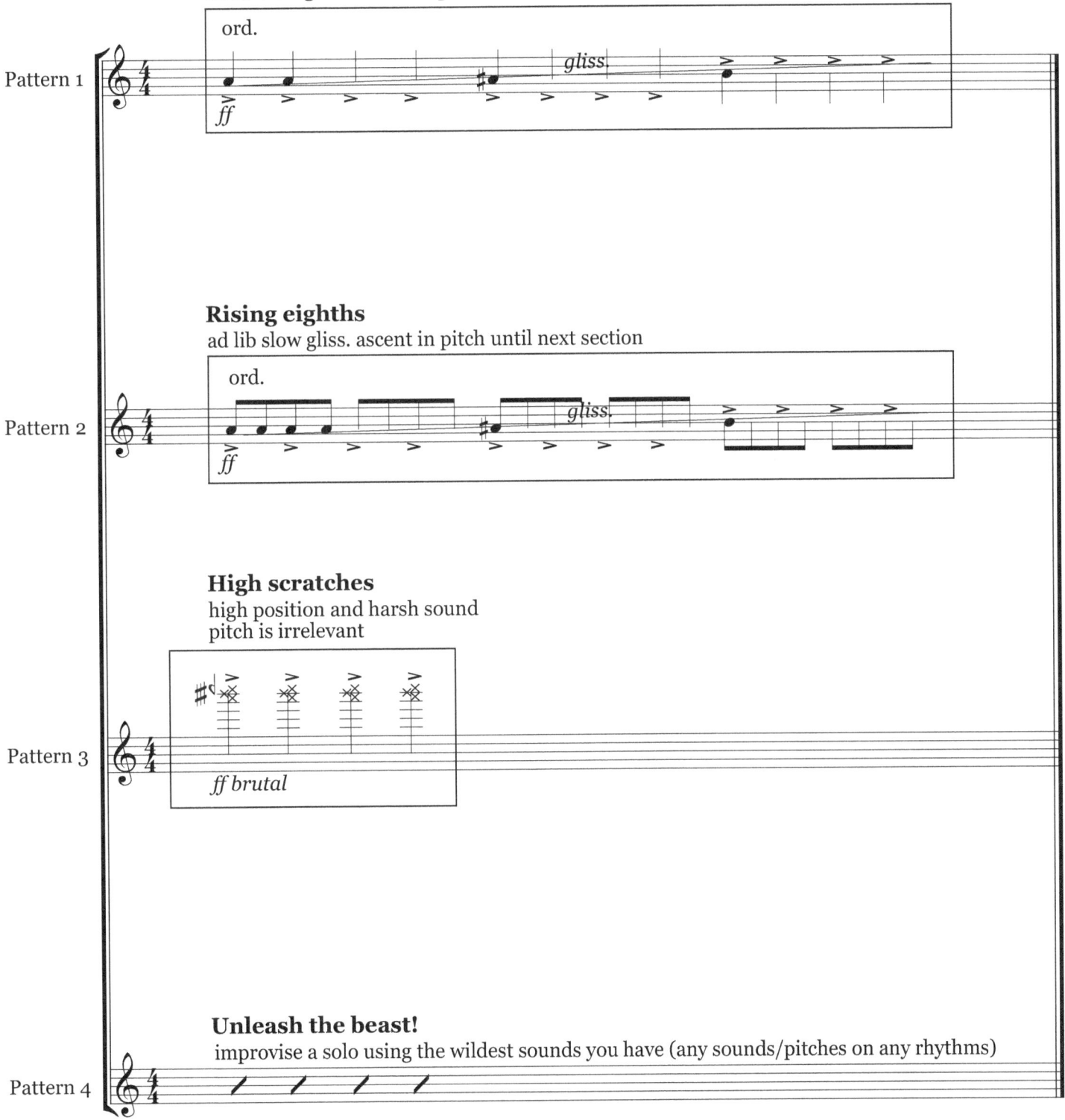

Rising quarters
ad lib slow gliss. ascent in pitch until next section

Rising eighths
ad lib slow gliss. ascent in pitch until next section

High scratches
high position and harsh sound
pitch is irrelevant

Unleash the beast!
improvise a solo using the wildest sounds you have (any sounds/pitches on any rhythms)

Thrust Into Chaos

The battle rages, a symphony of clashing steel and your own thunderous heartbeats. To your surprise, deep in the throes of brutal combat, the monster's rasping voice rings out in the echoey cavern.

"You are strong," it growls. You falter, dumbfounded; it can speak? Is this creature not a beast, but *intelligent*?

"It is good that you are strong," it affirms, lifting a golden locket from its neck and snapping the chain effortlessly. Wary, you begin to lift your sword, but all aggression seems to have evaporated from the monster's visage as it tosses you the locket. You lift a hand to receive it, as easily as in a game of catch with your younger siblings.

"Thank you," the monster says, its voice softening in gratitude, and again you are caught off guard. What if, perhaps, this creature isn't an enemy after all? But before clarity can take hold, an inky black explosion engulfs the cavern, and at its center a terrifying spectral presence looms. Your body stiffens, frozen in place, as the phantasm's voice explodes with fury: "Cael Mosshorn, your cursed existence ends now!"

Amid the swirl of smoke and mayhem, a violent lash surges from the putrid cloud enshrouding the demonic presence, and in one stroke obliterates the lower half of the scar-eyed monster you just faced. Trembling, you turn to face the spectral assailant alone, amid the growing wreckage of the cavern as it collapses under the destructive power of this assault. Its eyes meet yours, haunting orbs brimming with enmity and malevolence. With a razor-black whip again emerging from its shadowy core, this fearsome entity lashes you with a blow that entwines you in its grasp—not merely for this moment, you sense, but for all eternity, your destinies forever entangled. Simultaneously, you feel an inexplicable surge of acceleration sucking you forward into a void. Your vision blurs as your surroundings rush past at a dizzying speed, and you are drawn elsewhere, propelled into the unknown as the cavern crumbles into oblivion behind you.

Chapter Two

New Lands, New People

Anchorstone Harbor

When you emerge on the other side, a brilliant light engulfs you. Your vision, accustomed to the darkness of the cave, needs several rapid blinks to adapt. Bewildered, you gaze around at the unfamiliar cacophony of bustling commercial streets. As you inhale the damp, salty air, you feel a searing pain and look down to see a deep crimson stain blooming across your tunic. In an urgent plea for help you attempt to signal the harried passersby, but your equilibrium abandons you after a single step. You crumple to the ground. As your consciousness fades to black, you hear voices crying out in alarm and feel yourself lifted. You wonder if this is the end.

When you awaken, your eyes open to an unfamiliar ceiling. Before you even have time to consider whether you are alive or dead, a gentle, reassuring voice says, "Have no fear. You are in a place of safety." When you turn your head, you see a woman of quiet poise. "I am Arlith Rose," she says. You wonder if this is an intricate dream, and your sense of reality is blurred further as your eyes drift downward, anticipating the sight of your grievous wound. To your astonishment, however, there is no trace of injury.

"I healed you," she says simply. "That was a mortal wound; you nearly died." The revelation unfurls yet another perplexing tapestry of questions within you. But before you can ask for clarification, she holds up her index finger in evidence, a glint of iridescence dancing upon her nail. Drawing it lightly across the back of your hand, she raises a thin line of blood from beneath your skin. You gasp, but before you can feel pain, her hand, now entirely bathed in a faint turquoise glow, descends upon your own. A tingling sensation courses through you, and when you withdraw your hand, astonished, the wound has vanished. "I am a healer," she confirms. "I see that you doubt, but I assure you that magic—or rather, spirit energy—is undeniably real."

As you struggle to process this demonstration, she produces a locket. "Where did you get this?" she asks, searching your face with curiosity.

For a moment, you don't understand. Then the details of your battle come rushing back. You explain the circumstances through which the locket came into your possession.

"So you saw Cael," she concludes knowingly. "And the evil one. Oh... poor Cael. May he rest in peace." With a hand over her heart, Arlith blinks away tears. When her gaze finds you again she speaks simply, the gravity of her message ringing clearly through her steady words. "Cael was no monster. Rather, he was a hero, and sacrificed himself to defend the world from great evil. And now, whether you like it or not, you are bound to this unfinished battle to save the world."

The extraordinary narrative she spins is too implausible to accept at face value. But of the many questions you have, one rises to the forefront. You ask her why you have been drawn into this, your voice weighted with a mixture of doubt and frustration. She smiles in sympathy, but her voice is strong.

"My dear child, as he died Cael used the last vestiges of his spirit energy to throw you across space and time to this place, Anchorstone Harbor, where I could find you. It was a selfless act. In so doing he saved you from the clutches of the evil one called Void."

Her words are a revelation: you have become embroiled in an epic contest between good and evil, fought beyond the surface layers of the ordinary world.

"The wound inflicted by Void has not only marred your body," Arlith explains, "but has also left a scar upon your spirit energy. Recovery will be a difficult trial, a path filled with weakness and uncertainty," she warns." I can help, but only *you* can perform the feats that will ultimately restore you to wholeness."

Arlith softens, sensing in your tremulous silence the wish to go home, to return to the safe and familiar life you knew before all these truths undid everything you thought you understood about the world. But she presses on.

"Though I wish to be of help, I do not possess the ability of instant transport to aid you on this journey, as Cael did. The best I can offer is to provide you with shelter, training, and food. Take this day to regain your strength," she urges gently. "Tomorrow you can set off on foot to explore our sprawling city."

The next day, feeling renewed by your restful slumber and Arlith's nourishing food, you venture out into bustling merchant city of Anchorstone Harbor, eager to learn its unfamiliar cadence and rhythm. Yet the weight of unanswered questions presses upon you as you go: What lies ahead on this curious journey to wholeness that Arlith speaks of? How deep runs the danger that Void poses? And what of your beloved family of fellow orphans and dear Aunt Rowena back in Amberglade; will *they* be safe? And above all, there is the enigma of Arlith herself, a mysterious guardian harboring secrets you can scarcely fathom. But for now, with a jaunty spring in your step, you set your mind to exploring the city.

4. Anchorstone Harbor

Far away from home

Nick Revel

This new city sounds and feels so different from home. Can you learn to navigate its strange key and time signatures to gain comfort? Can you hear the Hero's theme in the Audio Play-Along?

Olde Baeworth's Tavern

After several days spent learning the intricacies of the city, you are just finishing a hearty breakfast at Arlith's table and preparing for another day out in the town when Arlith catches your gaze with a knowing smile. With a flick of her hand, she tosses you a glinting coin. "Have a meal at Olde Bae's today," she says playfully. "You may catch wind of relevant stories to help you in your journey." You pocket it with thanks; as aways, questions abound, but the allure of her suggestion proves irresistible.

From your reconnaissance of the city you know that Olde Baeworth's Tavern, a dingy dive not far from Arlith's dwelling, also doubles as an unofficial forum for tales and tidings. After a morning visiting the now-familiar haunts of the harbor and its surroundings, you pass through the brawl-battered doors of the tavern and pause, hit by the heady scent of aged ale and the salty tang of sweat. Despite the raucousness, the tavern's denizens exude an unmistakable camaraderie; besides, you're hungry and Arlith's coin is practically burning a hole in your pocket.

Navigating the boisterous crowd and deftly avoiding stray elbows, wayward stumbles, and the occasional puddle of spilled ale, you manage to secure the last remaining seat at a worn wooden table. Here, you intend to keep to yourself while you eavesdrop on conversations around you, as Arlith has recommended.

5. Olde Boeworth's Tavern

Nick Revel

Home to a boisterous crowd

Sharpening Your Skills

Amid the clamor of conversation and jovial bursts of laughter, you catch fragments of a tale that evokes a simmering anger within you. Its teller speaks of a wolf thrust into the Grand Coliseum of Raeganthia, a distant empire across the sea. The idea of forcing an animal to battle for the amusement of the masses is enough to make your stomach churn. How could Cael have sacrificed himself for the benefit of seemingly heartless people like these?

But as the chatter around you continues, it takes on a curious twist. Passing references to the wolf's speech confound your initial indignation. Could it be a talking dog; a creature touched by magic, perhaps a thread akin to those woven through Arlith's cryptic narrative? Though you are hesitant to betray your ignorance, curiosity compels you to inquire aloud about the identity of this mysterious wolf.

Your question elicits boisterous laughter from the crowd, and you try but fail to conceal your reddening face behind a pint of ale. They clarify that she is no canine, but rather a formidable warrior known as the Wolf, the most prized gladiator of the Coliseum. Her reputation is fearsome indeed; she is as fierce as the most savage beasts, battling in the arena for her patrons'—and her own— entertainment. With the haughty assurance of an unbeatable adversary, in each fight she wagers her ultimate asset: the Talaria, magical boots that afford her a speed unknown to man or animal. As far as anyone knows, she has never tasted defeat.

Now *this* is interesting, you think. When you ask aloud if such mystical footwear could aid someone in the pursuit of defeating Void, only blank expressions greet your query; no one seems to even recognize the term Void. Could they really be so ignorant of this looming threat? It seems that the world remains unaware of the peril it faces.

Thanking the strangers for the conversation and enduring their guffaws, you hurry back to Arlith, brimming with questions. She confirms the veracity of the tale.

"You see?" she says with a twinkle in her eye. "I knew you'd find out exactly what you needed to hear in Old Bae's." Then she turns serious. "Your mission, the first step along your path to recovery and working to counter Void," she announces, "is to train diligently, sharpening your skills until you're strong enough to face Wolf in the Coliseum." Your spine stiffens with resolve as you accept her charge. Daunting as it may seem, the care she has bestowed upon you, and the trust she demonstrates in your ability to make good on Cael's sacrifice, compels you to embrace this challenge.

The next morning, just after dawn, Arlith guides you to the training grounds on the outskirts of town. Setting aside her usual basket of healing herbs, Arlith demonstrates her prowess at various exercises that are designed to refine and enhance your abilities. A shiver of intimidation passes through you as you watch others training, aspirants to some unknown destiny, whose mastery looms far beyond your current level of ability. However, Arlith's reassuring presence soothes your apprehension as she imparts the fundamentals. She seems well versed in the arts of self defense. You can't help but voice your puzzlement, having believed her to be solely a healer.

But Arlith's response resounds with wisdom. "To rely on a single skill, no matter how great that skill, is to limit oneself. Adaptation to new situations requires a diverse arsenal of tools. Dedicate yourself to this regimen today, tomorrow, and every day for a week, and you shall witness the beginnings of transformation."

6.1 Training Grounds:
DragonScales 3 Octave Scales and Arpeggios

Nick Revel

Major Scales Excerpt

The rhythmic progression below corresponds to the audio play-alongs accessed via the above QR code. For all the scales, each bar in the progression represents one full cycle of the 3-octave scale. The first cycle is all half notes, the second cycle is all quarter notes, and so on. The original *DragonScales 3 Octave Scales and Arpeggios* book, from which this material is excerpted, contains a complete set of scales and arpeggios fully notated in slow to fast rhythms in all keys. Each key, contains six scales (Major, Minor, Whole Tone, two Diminished, and Chromatic) and two sets of arpeggios that progress through ten harmonies. To learn more or purchase the original DragonScales, visit www.nickrevel.com/dragonscales.

Rhythmic Progression

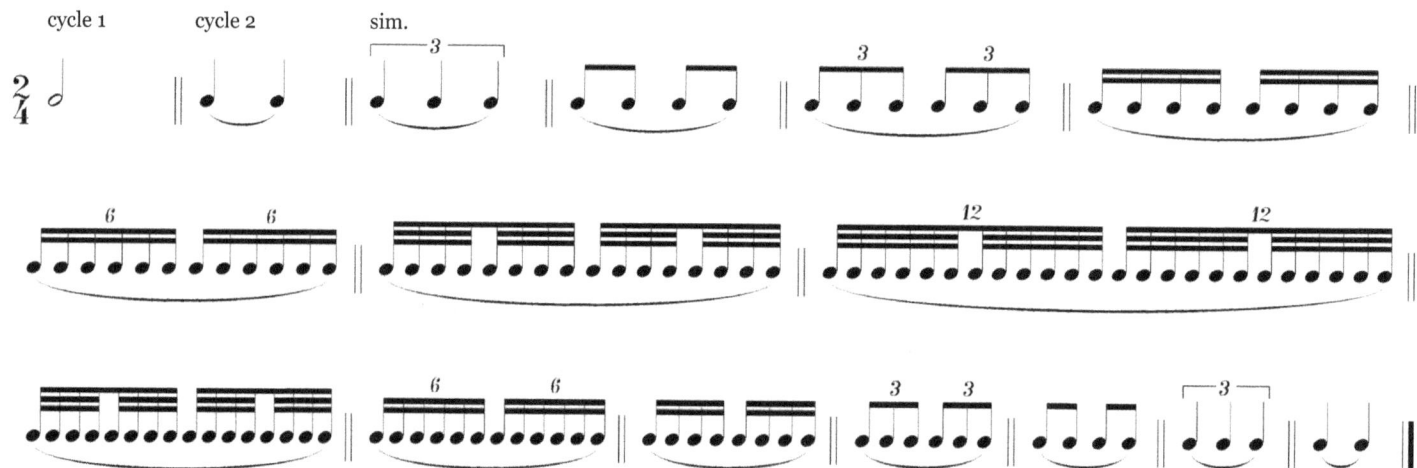

Here are some ideas to use this play-along:

1. Play in unison with the Audio Play-Along using the rhythmic progression above as a guide. If 3-octave scales are not available on your instrument, switch octaves when needed. Stay within your rhythmic comfort zone.
2. Experiment with dynamics, articulations, vibrato (width and speed), and tone.
3. Play in rhythmic unison with the play-along while playing only the root.
4. Play in diatonic intervals with the play-along by starting on different notes within the key signature.
5. Play in parallel non-diatonic intervals (minor 2nds, Major 2nds, minor 3rds etc...).
6. Sing the key signature's root while playing in unison with the play-alongs.
7. Create your own methods for using the audio play-alongs.

6.2 Training Grounds:
Meter and Rhythm

Nick Revel

This etude presents a series of metric modulations. You can hear both staves in the audio play-along. The tempos for each modulation, as well as the rhythmic conversions, are given at every change. The track repeats once, giving you the opportunity to try again or play the other staff.

Here are some ideas to use this play-along:

1. While listening to the audio play-along, tap, drum, speak, or play on any pitch the top staff.
2. Tap, drum, speak, or play on any pitch, each of the lines in the lower staff.
3. Once comfortable with the rhythm, expriment with note choice in either staff.
4. For an added challenge, tap your foot on the beat, not the rhythm, while you play.
5. For an extreme challenge, assign and play different pitches to all three lines in the bottom staff.

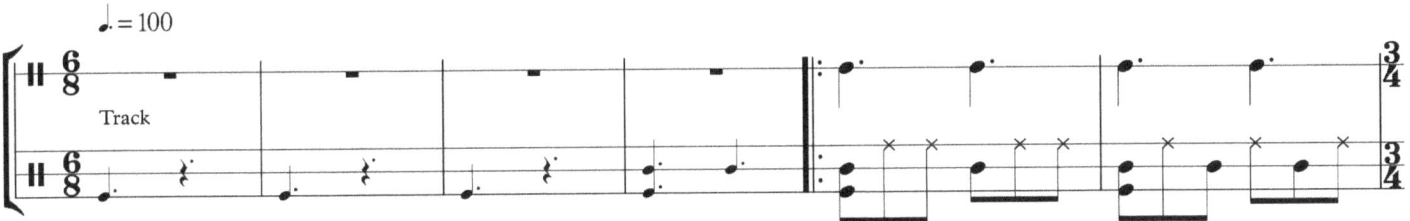

Unlock this level in
NOBLE
difficulty

6.3 Training Grounds:
Finding Harmony

Nick Revel

Triads
3-Note chords built with stacked 3rds

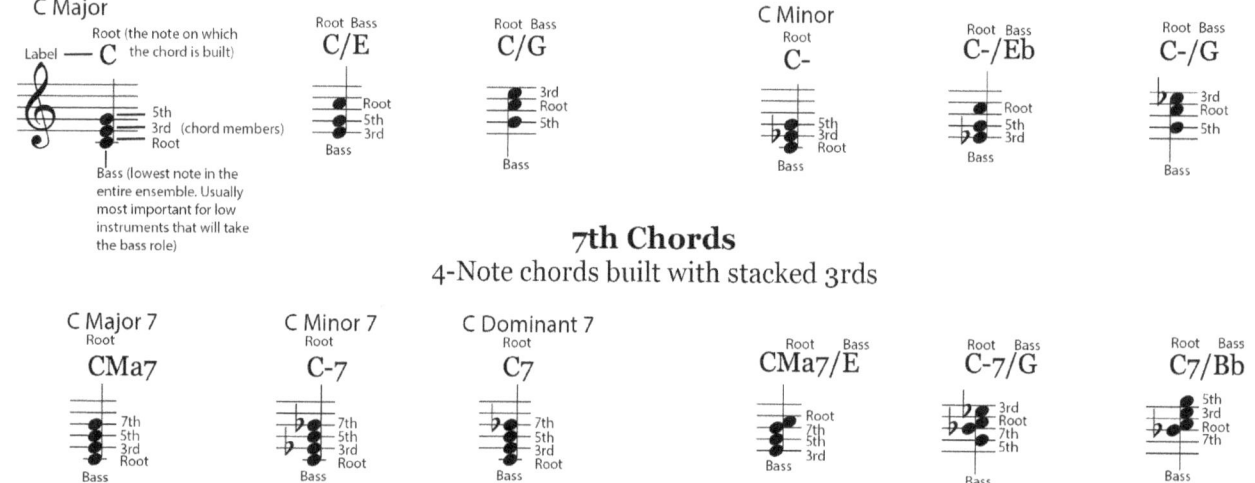

7th Chords
4-Note chords built with stacked 3rds

Label the chords and their members

Play
Audio Play-along: "6.3 Finding Harmony 1"

1. Arpeggiate the chords on your instrument in any comfortable tempo, rhythm, and register. An example is given.

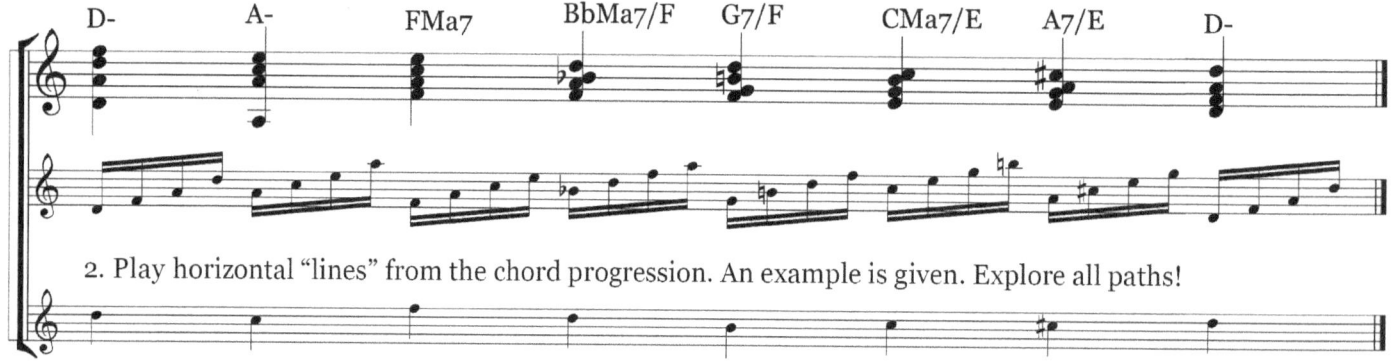

2. Play horizontal "lines" from the chord progression. An example is given. Explore all paths!

1. Fill in the missing labels and notes from the progression.
2. Arpeggiate the chords on your instrument in and comfortable tempo, rhythm, and register.
3. Play horizontal lines from the chords.

Compose

1. Write and label your own chord progression using triads and seventh chords. You do not have to know how it will sound while writing. It does not have to sound "good". It is an exercise in building chords.
2. Bring your compositions to your friend or teacher and play through them together, assigning one person to arpeggiate and the other to play horizontal lines.

The Night Market

As Arlith observes your last day of training, she fixes you with a discerning gaze. When you finish, you move to join her, sweaty but satisfied. She congratulates you warmly for the hard-fought progress you've achieved, her face aglow. With unwavering confidence she declares you ready for the forthcoming journey across the vast seas to Raeganthia.

But before setting sail, she informs you, a crucial task awaits: this evening you must venture to the Night Market, a place of murky secrecy where armor, weapons, and potions can be acquired. Under the cover of darkness and shrouded in black cloth, you will peruse its wares in anonymity. These concealing measures are necessary, for the Night Market attracts dark spirit energy, and to be identified could betray your presence to the lurking Void.

Curiosity piques you, and you ask if your existence under normal circumstances is otherwise invisible to Void. With a patient air, Arlith explains how Void's connection to the human world remains tenuous due to the intricacies of spirit energy. "Spirit realms and our physical dimension exist as separate planes of existence," she says. "His inability to materialize and hunt for you in the human realm stems from the inherent nature of spirit energy. Whether light or dark, a spirit struggles to maintain physical form in our world, and even brief excursions into our dimension result in the swift erosion of the spirit's consciousness. The very fact that Void forced his way through the dimensional barrier and attempted to end your life after extinguishing Cael's highlights your profound significance in this battle, as it likely exacted a tremendous toll on Void's spirit force."

You take in the meaning of her words solemnly. But something has been puzzling you, and you ask how the two of you will be able to confront Void if he lacks a physical form.

Arlith's response is stark, revealing the harrowing nature of your quest. "Not 'we,' but 'you,' my child. *You* will ultimately face Void once you have obtained the Sacred Spirit Crystal, a conduit capable of projecting your consciousness and spirit energy beyond the dimensional barrier into the realm of Void. There, your final confrontation awaits. The journey to that moment will be fraught with learning and trials. For a moment, a shadow seems to cross her face. "But that is far off," she concludes, with a wave of her hand. "For now, your mission lies within the depths of the Night Market."

Once darkness has fallen upon the city and the urban symphony has fallen into hushed serenity, it is time. Arlith outfits you with a black robe, a face mask of cloth, and a small pouch brimming with golden coins. Suggesting certain items to look for, her slender fingers reach into her pocket to hand you a map, faded ink tracing a delicate line leading to the Night Market's hidden entryway.

You thank her and reaffirm your commitment to stealth, pulling the mask over your face and venturing from her door when the coast is clear. Following the line on the map down three squares, over the bridge, past the gate, and then left into an alley, you make haste with the furtive grace of a cat. As you step through the clandestine entrance and navigate the makeshift stalls of various merchants, your senses are alert to any deception or danger. The shadowy vendors' stalls bear wares both of authenticity and artifice. However, Arlith's wise counsel resonates within you, guiding your discerning eye toward the genuine treasures you seek.

7. Night Market

A treasure trove of exotic goods

Nick Revel

Wearing your cloak and hood, you try to blend into the mysterious Night Market. Can you fit into the changing harmonies by following the musical patterns through difficult key signatures?

Stepping Into the Unknown

The following morning, you proudly display your acquisitions to Arlith, who inspects your treasures with a sagely nod. Among the items is a vial, apparently unremarkable, the label simply bearing the words "Amaranth Dew." You'd purchased it only at Arlith's urging, its cost more than all your other bounty combined. Puzzled, you inquire now about its purpose.

Picking up the vial with care, Arlith tells you that this elixir possesses the unique power to materialize your ineffable spirit energy into a tangible physical form. Its efficacy, she explains, hinges on the inherent purity of your spirit energy. However, its use is deeply draining to both body and spirit. As such, it is to be used as a last resort, in emergencies only.

In spite of your care for your anonymity, the previous night's venture into the Night Market casts a shadow of concern about your continued presence in this city. Thus Arlith, perceptive as ever, decrees that it's time for you to embark on your journey to Raeganthia and meet your destiny with Wolf. A ship known as the *Pearlwood,* she informs you, has been enlisted for your five-day odyssey across the sea. On this treacherous journey your mettle will be tested, as in exchange for your passage you must shield both the ship and its captain from the perils lurking beneath the waves.

Having related the particulars of your itinerary, Arlith's demeanor softens as she reflects on your time together. "Your presence has been a cherished gift," she admits, "and I wish you strength in your coming journey. Your path ahead is fraught with trials, and while I regret that fate has thrust them upon you, I urge you to embrace them with the valor of a hero. Have faith in yourself, for it is through your resolve that you will eventually find your way back to Amberglade."

A sharp note of curiosity punctuates your thoughts. How can a woman who took you in on a remote and unknown shore know of your origins and upbringing? Puzzlement tinges your voice as you ask her how much she *really* knows about you.

Her reply, though cryptic, carries the promise of revelations yet to come: "In due time, the full nature of your path will be revealed. For now, know in your heart that thus far you have exceeded expectations. Fare well upon your journey, dear one. May the spirits of light watch over you."

Chapter Three
The Wide Open World

Churning Seas

Life at sea proves to be a most unwelcome adventure. The perpetual swaying of the ship, amplified during tempestuous storms, subjects you to unending bouts of violent seasickness. Struggling to maintain a semblance of equilibrium, you wage a constant internal battle against the relentless pitching of the vessel. When the storms abate, windless days halt your progress and leave you drifting listlessly on the waveless sea, fearing that sheer boredom may part you from your sanity. Ironically, despite your devoted efforts in the training grounds preparing to defend the crew in case of a subaquatic attack, you find that the monstrous threats lurking beneath the waves pale in comparison to this ceaseless discomfort.

8. Churning Seas

A long voyage begins

Nick Revel

I. Open Seas Captain's Log Day 1: Setting sail, fresh breeze, crisp air. First sea voyage for young hero.

II. Doldrums

Captain's Log Day 2: No wind, too hot, smells of old fish. Young one seems bored.

♩ = 60

Track Vamp

Explore playing, clapping, or singing these small puzzles over the unchanging Vamp

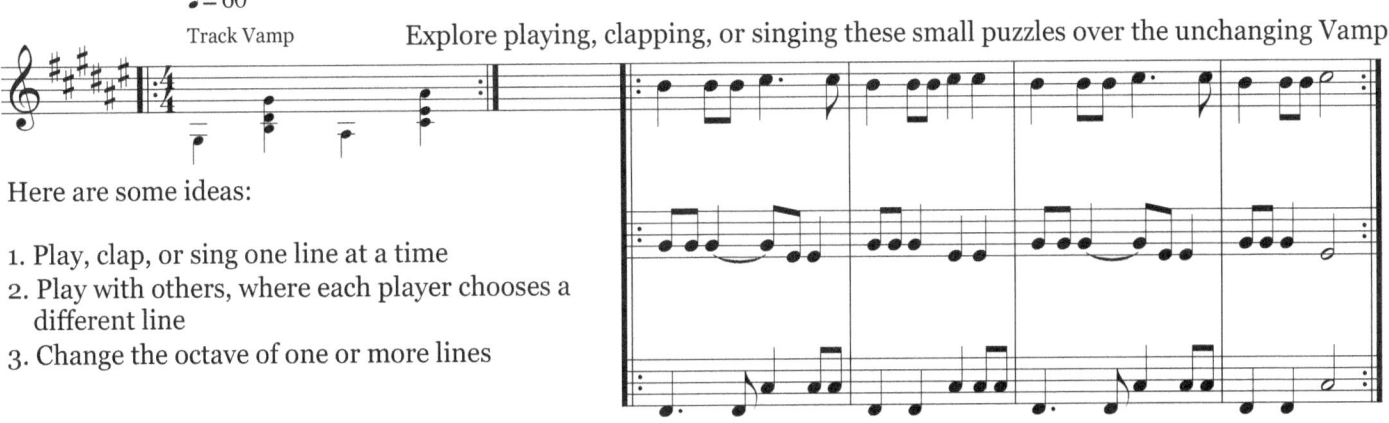

Here are some ideas:

1. Play, clap, or sing one line at a time
2. Play with others, where each player chooses a different line
3. Change the octave of one or more lines

1. Play, clap, or sing one line at a time
2. Play with others, where each player chooses a different line
3. Play only 16th notes where they occur to combine them into a single line of 16th notes

1. Sing or play the top line (G#→A#)
2. Sing or play the other lines (ex. D#→E# etc...)
3. Play with others, where each player chooses a different line

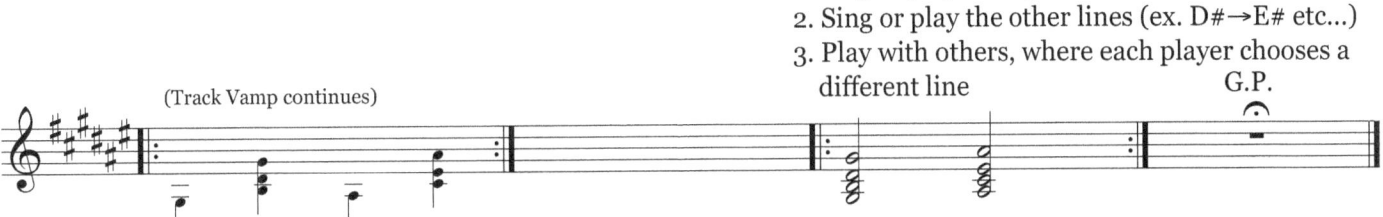

III. Tempest

Captain's Log Day 3: Black clouds and lightning, sharp winds, a storm brews. Brace! I pray she lets us out...

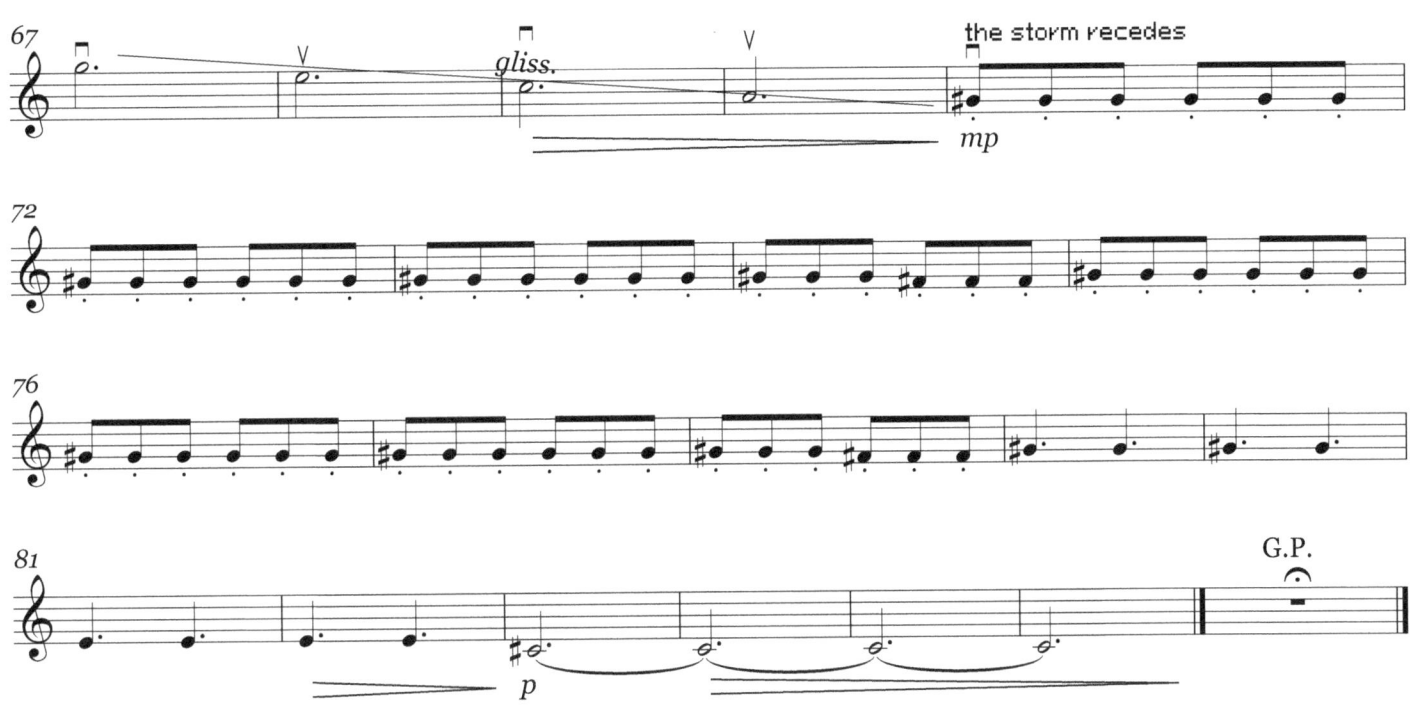

IV. Nausea

Captain's Log Day 4: Survived the storm. We rock in afterstorm wakes. Young hero is going through it...

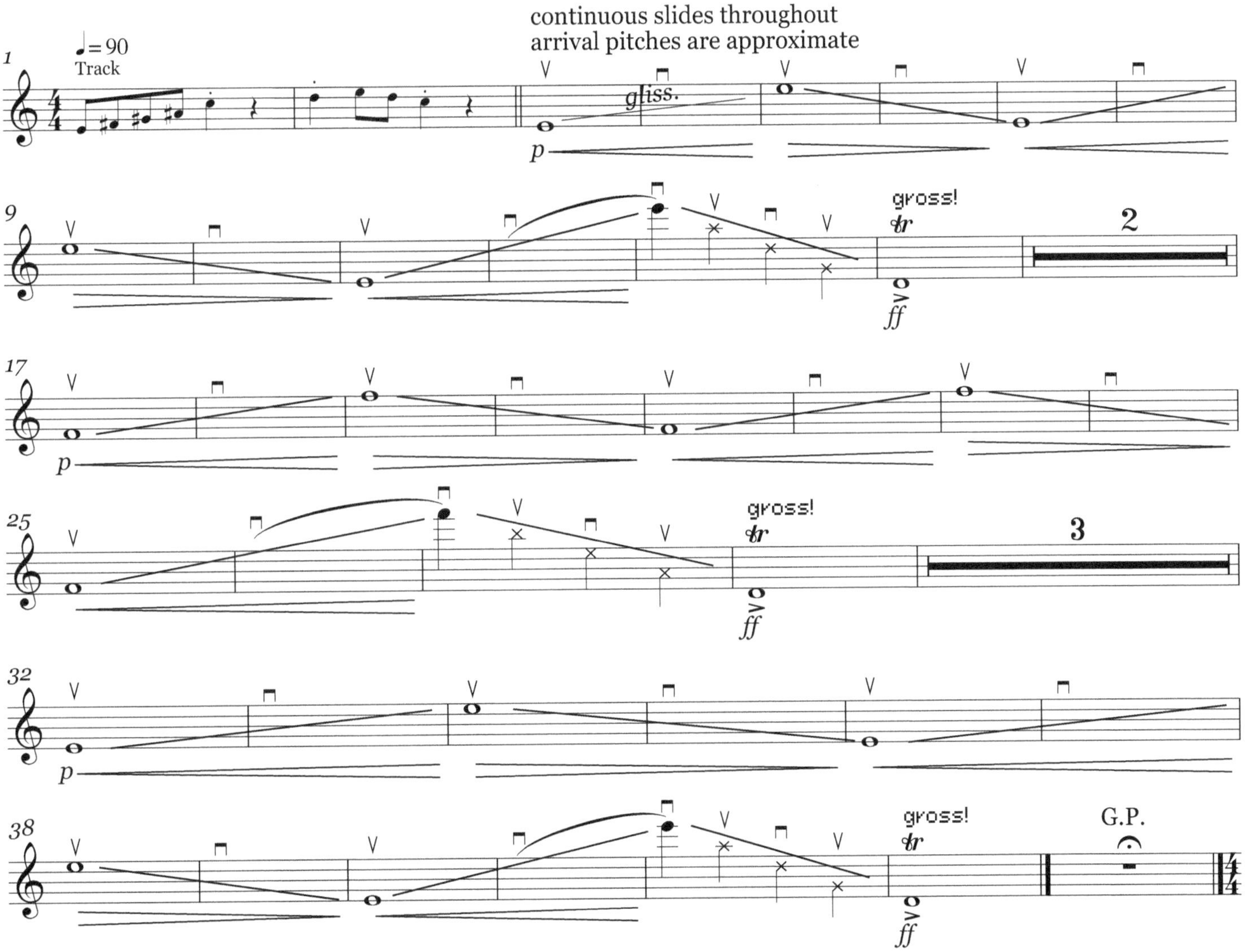

continuous slides throughout
arrival pitches are approximate

V. Battle

Captain's Log Day 5: Young hero is amazing! Battles fiercesome sea monsters. Eerily still when they retreat below surface.

Empire City Raeganthia

At long last, after enduring five grueling days and nights on the open sea, you find yourself at the formidable gates of Raeganthia. Never before have your eyes feasted upon such a spectacle of grandeur. Imposing structures fashioned from pristine, white stone ascend skyward, their surfaces glistening brilliantly in the rays of sunlight. Ornate decorations of pure gold adorn the stern governmental edifices.

Yet it is the Coliseum, this city's crowning jewel, that stands as the epitome of public extravagance, its immense, rounded form setting it apart from the rest. Here, you know, awaits the storied Wolf, lurking somewhere within. Arlith has provided you with directions, but the tantalizing allure of Raeganthia's architectural splendor beckons you to wander its streets, so boundless and labyrinthine you might easily lose yourself in its mesmerizing expanse. Perhaps, you think, you'll snatch a bit of further information about the Wolf that could come in handy in the days to come.

9. Empire City Raeganthia

Nick Revel

Sprawling grandeur

STOP! Do not attempt to play this etude! Instead, follow the instructions on the next page.

Glossary

Repeat Bar: At the second set of two dots, warp back to the first set of two dots.

1st ending: Take this the first time through a repeated section. Follow the repeat bar.

2nd ending: Take this the second time through a repeated section. Do not repeat. Continue out of the section.

Coda: The tail of the piece.

Coda 2: The second tail of the piece! This is very rare.

Segno: The warp marker tells you where to warp back to later in the piece. Remember where it is!

Serpent: At the second Serpent warp back to the first Serpent. Do this only once.

Double serpent: After following the Serpent, at the first Double Serpent, warp to the second Double Serpent.

Capo	The top of the piece.
D.S. al Coda	Warp back to the Segno (do you remember where?) and at the Coda, warp to the Coda.
D.C. al Coda 2	Warp back to the Capo and at the double Coda, warp to the Coda 2.
D.S. al Fine	Warp back to the Segno and at the word "Fine", stop playing. You've made it!

Raeganthia is a confusing place! Luckily Arlith has given you a map to navigate it. Can you decipher the musical symbols and follow the steps below to find Wolf?

1. Use the Glossary on the previous page and find each of the terms and symbols in the etude printed above.

2. Below is the map Arlith gave you. The symbols on each signpost (1-20) tell you which part of the piece to play next. In the numbered spaces below, fill in the bar numbers you will travel through before the next signpost. (In this piece, 1st and 2nd endings have separate bar numbers.) Remember that Segnos, Codas, and Fines are only taken the second time through a section!

3. Look at the part while listening to the Audio Play-Along recording and see if you can follow along!

1 1-12

2 5-11

3 13-

4 _____

5 _____

6 _____

7 _____

8 _____

9 _____

10 _____

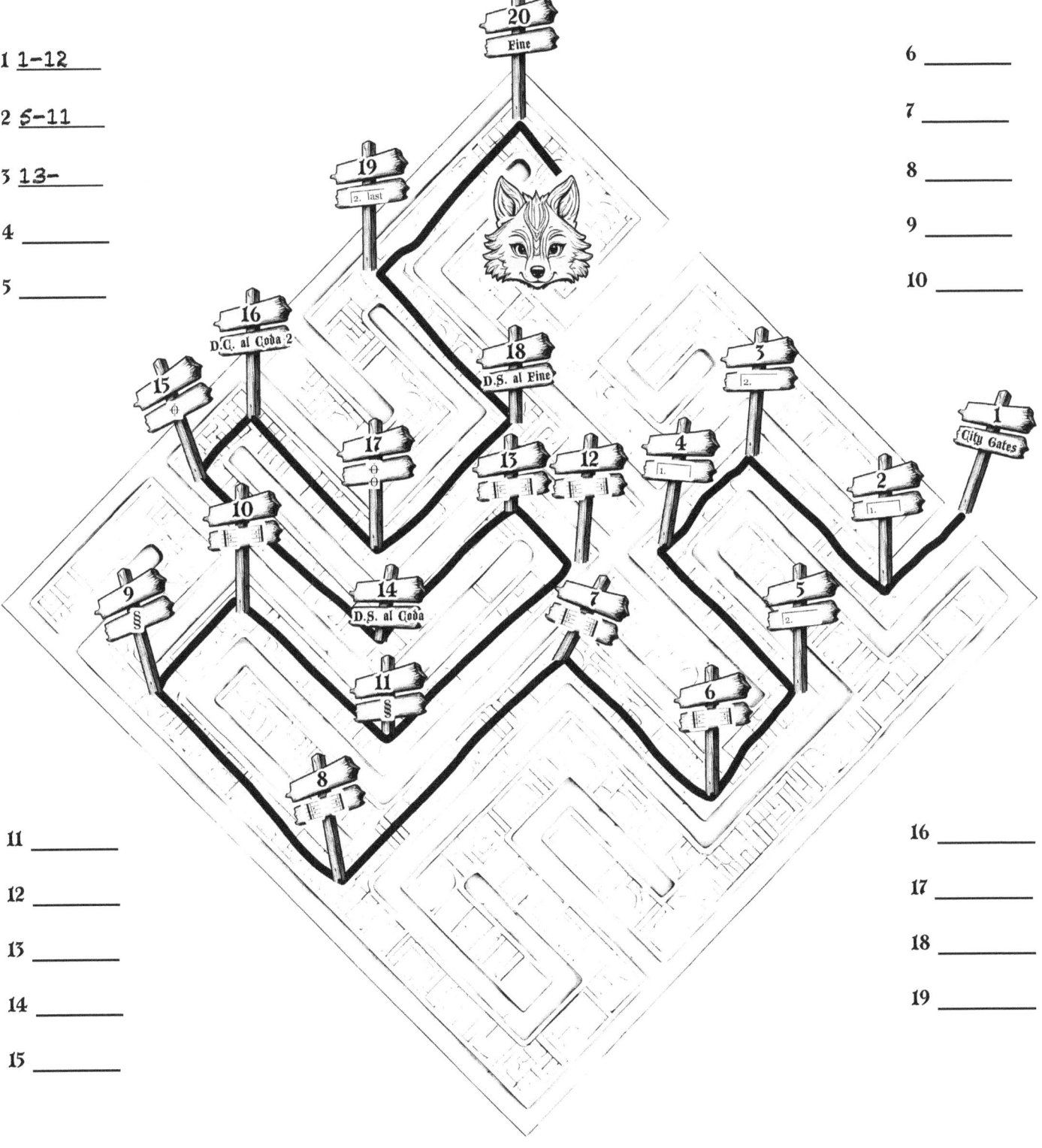

11 _____

12 _____

13 _____

14 _____

15 _____

16 _____

17 _____

18 _____

19 _____

Answers:

1. 1-12
2. 5-11
3. 13-21
4. 14-20
5. 22-24
6. 24-25
7. 25-26
8. 26-28
9. 24
10. 24
11. 29
12. 29-30
13. 30-32
14. 14-20
15. 33-57
16. 5-11
17. 58-74
18. 14-20
19. 22-23

Hunted By a Wolf

After hours of wandering amid the grandeur of the city, you have learned nothing of value to add to your intelligence about Wolf. Dejected and about to give up, you turn a corner and collide head-on with what you initially mistake for a stone statue. You rub your smarting forehead, cursing under your breath, when—to your bewilderment—this seemingly inanimate figure springs to life. Its transformation into a living, breathing woman is as astonishing as it is disconcerting. She meets your surprised expression with a sly smile, a devilish gleam flashing in her silver eyes, which seem to peer into the depths of your soul.

A shiver courses down your spine as uncertainty engulfs you; should you flee or confront this intimidating stranger? But before you can decide, she lunges forward, and in one swift, powerful motion she pins your feet to the ground with hers and secures both your wrists with an iron grip.

"I'm Wolf," she declares, her teeth bared in a grin. "You and I will be battling in the Coliseum tomorrow." Her words pass through you like a jolt of electricity, crackling with anticipation. "I've heard some things about you," she continues. "You're the one who blazed through Anchorstone's training grounds with record-breaking prowess. Earned quite the reputation," she scoffs, lifting her furry eyebrows. Then her eyes narrow, focused. "I'm looking forward to our match tomorrow. And in case you didn't know, if you can snatch my pendant, you'll earn these," she taunts, pointing down to her coveted boots, the Talaria. Then she leans in, her low voice becoming a growl. "I've been waiting for you. You'd better not let me down."

With a shove, she releases you and quickly turns the corner. But when you rush to follow her, you find nothing but empty air. Sinking to your knees to catch your breath and slow your racing heart, you contemplate the swirling mix of dread and determination in your stomach.

Sleep eludes you that night, and your stomach is too jittery for food. Morning dawns with a sense of impending doom as you equip yourself with your goods from the Night Market and make your way to the Coliseum. When you arrive, you behold a seemingly endless line of spectators stretching out before you. Upon inquiring about the contestants entrance, you discover that you're already in the correct line: dozens upon dozens await their chance to challenge Wolf, driven by the promise of honor and the magical Talaria.

At long last, a thunderous roar emanates from the Coliseum, signaling Wolf's entrance. The atmosphere immediately electrifies, hushed murmurs rippling through the line as the crowd in the arena responds to Wolf's feats of devastation. One by one, contestants enter the Coliseum, only to be swiftly vanquished. Anxiety churns in your gut, futile desperation echoing through your mind. How can you possibly defeat her?

The minutes and hours blur as you wait, paralyzed with fear, and before you know it you find yourself escorted into the open ground of the Coliseum. Wolf's piercing silver eyes fixate on you, her tanned, scarred frame emanating an aura of raw power. She beckons you closer, and, leaning in amidst the cacophony of the crowd, she turns her lupine face to your ear and sneers, "I'm bored. Entertain me."

A fist bump initiates the contest, followed by a hasty retreat into your respective corners. Wolf brandishes her pendant, a taunting gesture that kickstarts your fighter's instincts. The crowd's deafening clamor becomes a distant hum as your focus narrows to her fearsome countenance.

A gong's resonant tone marks the commencement of the duel.

In the initial exchange, you manage to hold your ground, trading blows evenly. Surprisingly, you keep pace with her, your confidence growing with each attack. However, amid the grunting and clashing of steel, a subtle realization dawns upon you; every time you approach, she effortlessly parries your strike within only millimeters. She's toying with her prey, letting you wear yourself out.

Eventually she tires of it. "You disappoint me, young warrior," she says with flat disdain. Fluidly activating her genuine speed and power, she lunges at you, and her broad shoulder connects with your chest, hurling you across the ring. The impact with the ground steals your breath, leaving you gasping for air as you tumble into a heap.

Your vision blurs, and a foreboding seizes you, as real as death; her next blow will be your last chance. Wolf stalks toward you. In your mind, Arlith's advice rings out: *"Only drink it in an emergency."* Surely this qualifies: if you fail to survive this battle, your quest to stop Void will come to naught. Watching Wolf advance, your eyes widen in terror. With trembling hands, you grab for the small bottle of Amaranth Dew in your pouch and hastily consume its contents. The overpowering sweetness of the elixir is accompanied by a tingling sensation, which warms your stomach. Heat rapidly spreads throughout your body until it begins scalding you from the inside. Your mind races; will you meet death in the end not with a beating, but with a burning?

10. Coliseum

Nick Revel

Staring into the Wolf's sharp silver eyes

Wolf is a fierce enemy! To defeat her, you'll need to learn to predict her moves. Listen to the Audio Play-Along and follow the score to learn where she moves next.

1. Learn the form of the piece: Use your ears to learn when to go from A Section to B Section and back. You can go by feel or write the form in bar numbers per section or loops per section.
2. Learn and play each pattern below in each section.
3. Once mastered, play with others, where each player chooses a different line.

A Section
(crowd cheers)

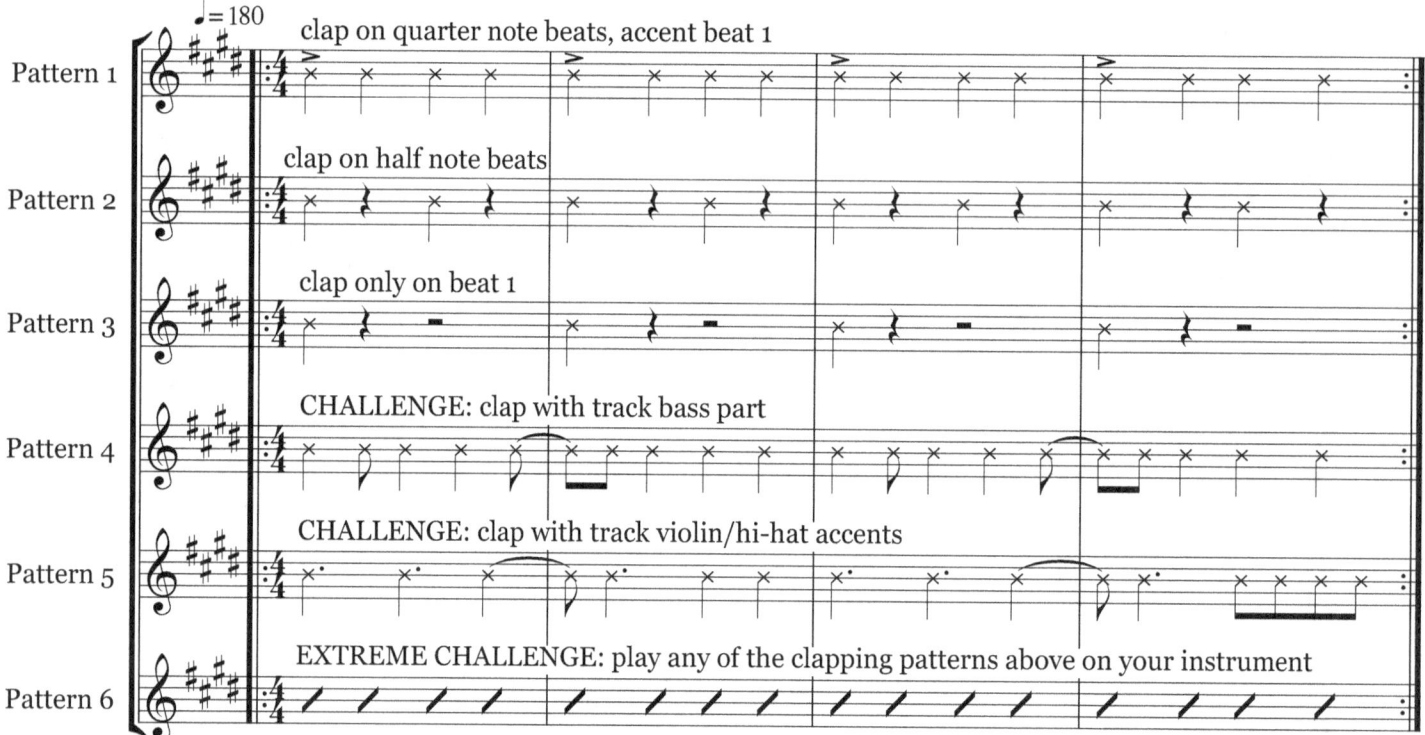

B Section
(epic beat drop)

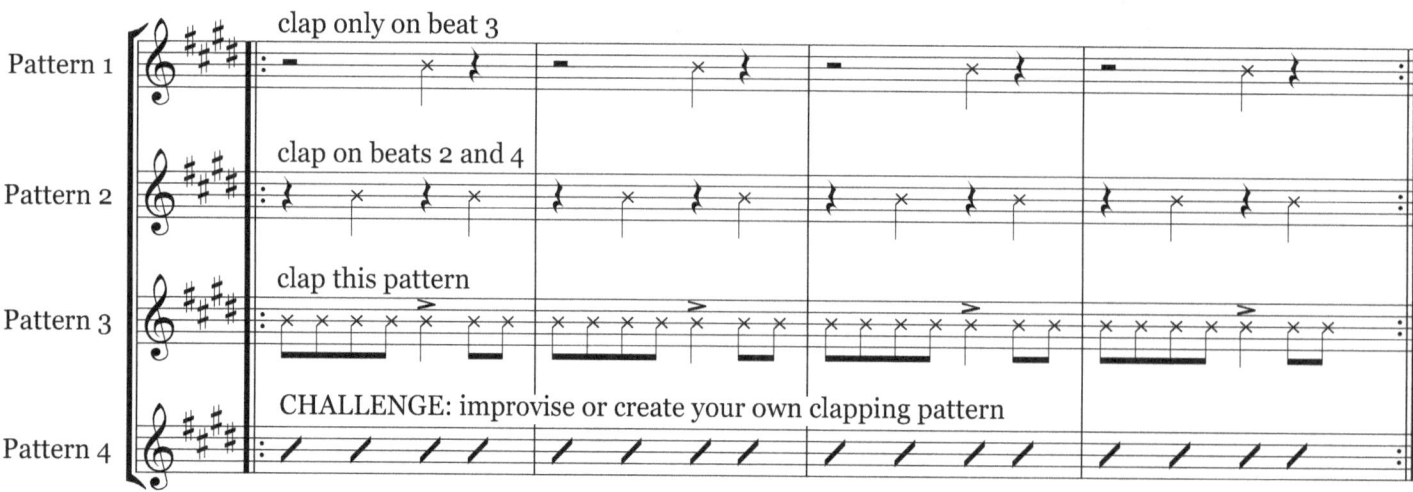

Optional B Section Challenge Round

play along with the track bass part

play along with the main theme

play along with the counter theme

Truth Revealed

Electrifying sensations course through your limbs until an explosion of brilliant white light erupts from your very core. Just before the abyss of unconsciousness claims you, you witness Wolf propelled upward through the air by this mysterious, violent blast. All goes dark.

As consciousness slowly returns to you, you find yourself lying in a bed, grappling with the fog of fragmented memories. Opening your eyes, you absorb the sterile surroundings of the infirmary around you. From across the room, Wolf's gaze pierces through your still-hazy senses.

"Well, well, kid. You're stronger than you look. No human has *ever* inflicted such damage on me," she sneers, her tone a mix of reluctant admiration and disbelief. Your horrified gaze takes in her battered form in the bed opposite yours, swathed in splotchy red bandages, a testament to the chaos unleashed when you consumed the potion and sent an explosive shockwave outward.

"You really did a number on me and the Coliseum, which is now off-limits due to structural damage," she continues. Taking in your disbelief, she scoffs, "Do you even remember what happened?"

Hazily, you recount how you drank the Amaranth Dew and subsequently lost control over your body and its energy. Her nod carries the weight of understanding. "You almost offed yourself as well, you know. The limits of a body's ability to contain spirit energy are finite. Regardless, you won fair and square," she admits. "This is yours now."

She unclasps the chain on her pendant and, with a casual toss, flings it in your direction. When it lands in your upturned palm, you see that it's not a pendant at all in fact, but another locket, not unlike the one given to you by Cael Mosshorn just before his demise at the hands of Void. "Open it," she instructs. As you fumble with the locket, you try to assuage the guilt weighing heavy on your chest with an apology for her injuries, but she interrupts you. "Open it," she insists, steering the conversation away from your remorse.

Ceding to her command, you open the locket to reveal a miniature painting within, depicting younger versions of Wolf and Arlith. A figure you don't recognize stands beside them, as do two individuals whose faces are strangely familiar. Before you have time to think, your heart lurches with a premonition; could these be your long-lost parents?

With awe, you speechlessly drink in the image. Slowly the puzzle pieces align, and Arlith's prior cryptic remarks take on new significance. All at once a bevy of questions spills out of you into the tranquil hush of the infirmary: Who were your parents, how did they know Wolf and Arlith, who or what exactly is Void? And, most pressing of all, why have you been drawn into all this?

"All right, kid. Here's what you need to know," Wolf begins, her silver eyes focusing on the distance as if looking into the past. "As far as we know, Void is an ancient entity, born eons ago. He seeks to destroy humanity with something called the Dark Spirit Crystal. The five of us united to vanquish him," she says, pointing toward the locket. "We used the Sacred Spirit Crystal as our medium, but we weren't strong enough." As bitterness pervades Wolf's voice, you steal another glance at the miniature faces arrayed inside the locket, counting them. Wolf and Arlith, to be sure, and your parents, which Wolf has not denied. But who is this fifth figure, a robust, bearded young man looking out from the portrait with kind eyes?

Wolf's fierce eyes soften. "Poor Cael. All we managed to do was seal Void temporarily in his own realm, and in a final act of retaliation he inflicted a terrible curse on Cael. Poor guy became a living monstrosity. All of us were so broken by the end, and your parents...." Her voice falters, laden with grief. "They didn't make it." She brushes away a tear and sighs. "Cael knew he could never live among humans again and went into hiding in the cavern. And the Sacred Spirit Crystal, our most powerful weapon, fell into the hands of Nythrag, Void's mightiest disciple. That beast still possesses it to this day. Your parents' wishes, written down in case of the unthinkable, entrusted you to Rowena's orphanage in Amberglade." She pauses, letting you process the facts. "And the worst part," she snarls, "is that these ungrateful humans know nothing of our sacrifice. Now you know why I take out my rage in the Coliseum every day."

She lets this sink in for a moment, then continues, her tone growing more urgent. "The barrier between realms is weakening now, and Void isn't only out to get us, he wants to destroy humanity itself. Like it or not, your parents' sacrifice means that only you can defeat Nythrag to retrieve the Sacred Spirit Crystal. You'll have to beat down some seriously nasty beasts along the way. It's a daunting path, to be sure, but you've already shown how strong you are," she banters, gesturing a hand over her battered body.

"But anyway, we're safe for now, as Void is most likely still recovering from his contact with the physical realm when he killed Cael. So now it's time to blow off some steam. You need time to heal, anyway. Have you heard about the Moonlight Masquerade yet? It is an event of *unparalleled* beauty and extravagance," she says with mock ostentation. "You should go and have yourself a good time. You never know who might meet." She winks.

After several days of rest in the infirmary, you find yourself wondering whether you can possibly be healed in time to attend the festival, let alone face the perils that lie ahead. While both you and Wolf have been drinking healing potions for days, no mortal concoction could compare to Arlith's abilities, and you wish she was there to assist you. Suddenly there is a knock at the door; the infirmary door swings open, and there, with her comforting air of grace and wisdom, stands Arlith. Without a word of greeting she immediately heads to Wolf and lays her hands over her wounds, capably healing her within minutes. An embrace follows, the reunion of old companions.

"Hello, my friend. Oh, how I've missed you," Arlith finally declares warmly, taking in Wolf's familiar visage. She then approaches you, her eyes brimming with concern. "I can mend your physical wounds, but the use of the Amaranth Dew has left your spirit energy depleted, and I cannot replenish your spirit reserves. Only time can do that," she explains gently. Once she has healed you, you sink deeper into the bed with relief. Her gifts have left you feeling better, but a deep exhaustion is threatening to overtake you. Weakly, you thank her and inquire about the particulars of her swift appearance in Raeganthia's infirmary, leagues across the stormy seas from her home in Anchorstone.

"Do you see the gem I wear around my neck, dear child?" She fingers it lightly. "It is a tiny spirit crystal, capable of sending micro amounts of spirit energy through time and space. Though they are not powerful enough to alter the physical universe, we can communicate through them; usually intentions and moods, although if we focus we can sometimes use words. When your spirit energy ruptured during your battle at the Coliseum, I felt it instantly through Wolf's crystal. Then came the five-day sea journey, which, trust me, was utterly dreadful." She shudders. "But here I am. And in the event that robust health comes to you in time for the festival, I did bring my most exquisite attire," she says with a hopeful smile. Wolf laughs raucously, breaking into a howl.

When the day of the festival dawns, you find yourself a little weary still, but in good spirits.

That evening, with Arlith in her finery and Wolf close at hand, you all venture forth into the hubbub. It proves an enchanting spectacle, with people from all walks of life congregating in celebration. Each reveler wears their finest formal clothing and a mask, the anonymity adding to the night's mystique.

Among this sea of masks and eyes, one figure stands out, captivating your attention with their lithe stature and enigmatic allure. Their graceful movements and haunting gaze spark a sudden thrill within and you find yourself blushing. Then, to your utter surprise, they approach, extending an invitation with a simple question: "Care to dance?"

Your heart pounding with anticipation, you accept. Let the revelry begin.

11. Moonlight Suite

It takes two

Nick Revel

This is a multi-player dance etude! The violin, viola, and cello are different but can all dance together.
The "solo" parts in the Audio Play-Along recordings are only in Noble and Legend modes.

I. Gavottesque

This blank page makes page turns easier

II. Intimate

Every good dance band needs a strong rhythm section...in this movement, that's you!
Can you hear all the drum patterns in the Audio Play-Along? Can you play along with each one of them,
using your hands and your instrument like a drum? Try playing one while your partner(s) plays the other(s).

III. Tarantella

The Real Test Begins

When you awake the next morning, memories of the Moonlight Masquerade and your exquisite dance partner whirling through your head, you realize that this profound connection, brief though it was, has deepened your appreciation for the sanctity of existence. This realization fuels your determination to safeguard life in all its forms.

After breakfast, Arlith and Wolf, the seasoned mentors of your nascent quest, supply you with your own communication crystal, and brief you on your forthcoming mission. First, you are to journey to Charnel Marsh, they inform you gravely, which no human has ever successfully passed through. There you will confront a vicious swamp monster named Necros, whose tentacled, squid-like form holds dominion over the desolate bog. Necros possesses one of the artifacts necessary to aid you in your defeat of Void, the mysterious Blur Stone, whose importance has not yet been explained to you. Acquiring the stone will be no easy feat: doing so will first entail evading the sinewy vines the demon uses to ensnare and suffocate its prey. To destroy the creature, you must go past them. The only way to significantly harm Necros, Wolf and Arlith explain, is by targeting its core body. The demon can swiftly regenerate its vines, which are coated in a viscous, lethal poison. A mere touch of the tentacles spells doom, as the poison will inexorably claim its victim. Worse still, the vast network of the Necros vines extends throughout the marsh's perimeter, and as the line between natural tree roots and the monstrous appendages blurs, identifying safe footholds is a formidable challenge.

When you despair, asking what could possibly help you beat such a demon, Wolf—her silver eyes gleaming—extends her Talaria boots toward you. "These," she declares. "With practice, these boots will grant you extraordinary agility, enabling superhuman speed to dodge the entwining vines. They alone can bring you close enough to the core of Necros to deliver decisive blows."

With gratitude and a heart bolstered by their faith, you accept the boots, and the weighty mission that lies ahead.

"May the spirits of light guide and protect you," Arlith intones, her voice brimming with earnest hope, as you prepare to venture deep inside the ominous heart of Charnel Marsh to meet the first of the three opponents between you and the Sacred Spirit Crystal.

Chapter Four
Slaying Evil

Charnel Marsh

Armed with confidence won from hard-earned skills and battle experience, and bearing four healing potions Arlith concocted specifically for you, you embark on the perilous journey into the Charnel Marsh to confront Necros. As you travel, you strive to fortify your resolve. As Wolf explained to you in the infirmary, the fate of the world hinges on your retrieval of the Sacred Spirit Crystal, guarded within the Obsidian Cavern by Void's most ruthless ambassador, Nythrag.

Your thoughts crowd with the impending danger, but you make a conscious effort to stay aware of the softening ground beneath your feet and the darkening canopy of decaying trees. As the Charnel Marsh unfolds before you, shrouded in an eerie fog, stagnant and still, emitting sickly-sweet odors of decay and death, your senses heighten, tingling with anticipation. As you pause, you sense Wolf's Talaria Boots begin to draw on your spirit energy, calling forth the reserves replenished by rest and Arlith's care. This very energy—finite, precious—will fuel your swift evasions from the lurking attacks of Necros with agile leaps to small footholds. You take a deep breath and enter the swamp: let the battle begin.

12. Necros

Use the Talaria Boots to quickly evade the lurking tentacles

You're in constant danger in this swamp! Can you avoid the lurking tentacles by making
swift and precise string crossings?

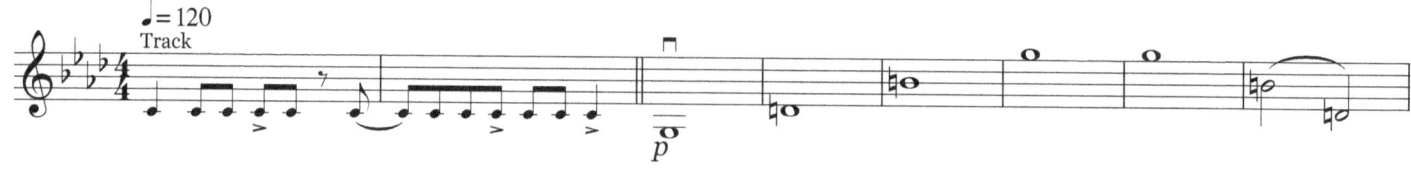

Optional simple part:

Optional simple part:

Optional simple part:

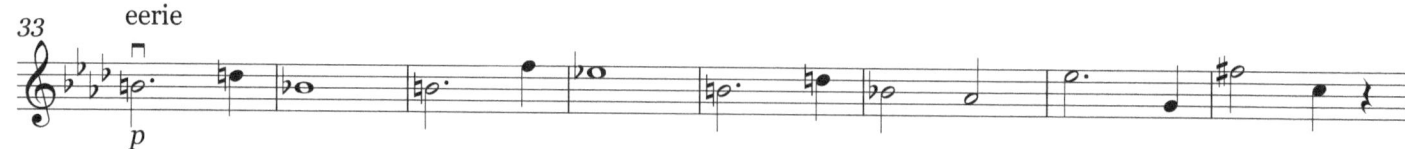

Battle at Wyrmcrest Peak

After an exhausting battle, you witness the grotesque spectacle of Necros's body dissolving into a primordial, viscous goo. Just as Arlith foretold, from this morbid gore emerges an unexpected treasure: a perfectly smooth and spherical stone, glistening with an otherworldly sheen. You retrieve the alluring stone from the muck, and as you rinse it in the water, a startling sensation washes over you, a feeling of your own presence diverging, oscillating between two forms simultaneously. This mysterious stone seems to possess the uncanny ability to blur your essence; novel and potentially useful, but palpably exhausting to your spirit energy. How dangerous might it be to carry for an extended period of time?

Just then, a familiar presence materializes through the communication crystal around your neck, and Arlith's soothing voice reaches out to you. "Well done, dear one. With your bravery you have retrieved the Blur Stone. As you have no doubt observed, using it must be done with awareness and caution, as it draws indiscriminately on your spirit energy, and thus the cost of employing it can be high. Be prudent in its use."

As you stow the stone carefully in a pocket, Arlith prepares you for the next encounter in your quest. Your second adversary is Haedus, a brutal and ferocious goat demon that patrols Wyrmcrest Peak, blocking entry to the Obsidian Cavern. With its blinding speed and the strength to crush rocks beneath its hooves, Haedus presents yet another daunting challenge. To prevail, you must learn to synchronize your spirit energy with the Blur Stone; this will enable you to deftly alternate between a normal state, when you can attack, and a flickering ethereal form, which will allow the demon's assaults to pass through you harmlessly. Victory will call for a delicate balance: your attacks will require moments of physical vulnerability, and therefore demand the utmost caution.

With Arlith's guidance echoing in your mind, you continue your journey through Charnel Marsh, heading toward the foot of Mount Wyrmcrest where a treacherous scramble up craggy peaks awaits you. Upon completing your ascent, you prepare to confront Haedus. Reaching into your pocket, you uncork and swallow one of Arlith's potions to restore the vital energy lost during the battle with Necros, and feel its potency rush through your body. Thus fortified, you sense the throb of the Blur Stone in your pocket as hoof-falls of the goat demon approach with alarming speed. Bring it on.

13. Haedus

Nick Revel

Synchronize your spirit energy with the Blur Stone to phase through the demon's ferocious attacks!

Total coordination is needed to avoid Haedus' attacks by masking your location!
Can you find these left hand rhythms and trills?

The Obsidian Cavern

As Haedus's once-fearsome form smolders, smokes, and falls to dust, leaving behind only his colossal horns and hooves, you collapse with exhaustion and relief. As the ashen remnants scatter, you reach into your pocket for Arlith's second potion and drink.

Arlith's voice chimes through the communication crystal again. "Dear one, our heartfelt congratulations on your hard-fought victory!" You can hear the sound of her smile beaming across the span of your separation. "What I tell you next will seem strange, but it is critical to your next step. Separately grind the tips of Haedus's horn and hoof into fine powders, and apply one to your upper eyelid and the other to your lower. The journey into the heart of the mountain through the Obsidian Caverns is treacherous; these dark passages harbor a sinister enchantment, a magical field that lulls any creature venturing within into an eternal slumber. The closer you approach the fabled treasure room where lies the coveted Chronospear, an essential weapon for vanquishing the ultimate and most perilous foe on your quest, the more potent the somnolent forces of the spell will become. The application of the horn and hoof dust to your eyelids and lashes will initiate a potent magi-chemical reaction, an adrenaline surge to keep you acutely alert in the face of the overwhelming pressure of slumber. However, should your eyelids close for more than three seconds, a secondary magi-chemical reaction between the two substances will occur, culminating in a sharp and painful jolt of energy through your eyes. Experiencing too many of these reactions will cause blindness.

"Only with the Chronospear can you succeed on your ultimate quest. But be forewarned, disturbing this precious artifact will trigger the awakening of Nythrag, the ultimate guardian of the Sacred Spirit Crystal. And your ultimate mission is to retrieve that crystal at all costs.

"As you embark on this perilous endeavor, heed my parting words: you must not succumb to the beckoning allure of slumber, no matter how tempting. The fate of all humanity rests on your ability to resist the enchanting call of eternal rest."

Thus fortified by Arlith's valediction, you prepare the special dust as instructed and ready yourself to venture into the dark heart of the Obsidian Caverns.

14. The Obsidian Cavern

Nick Revel

Keep your goal in sight. Resist the spell of eternal slumber!

This etude is like a dark cavern. Can you feel your way through it with some practice?
The A sections have no tempo or key...just interact with what you hear in the Audio Play-Along.
The other sections are in different tempos and use repeating patterns of notes. Can you hear these
patterns in the Audio Play-Along? Can you play along with them and find your way to the treasure room?

A Section, no tempo

interact with drip drops
improvise pizz or tapping sounds

Here are ideas for interacting with the B, C, and D sections:

1. Listen for the printed note patterns in the track
2. Say the pattern in numbers with the track (Ex. 1 2 3 4 5   1 2 3 4 5)
3. While counting the pattern, clap on the "1"
4. Notice when the speed of the pattern changes and adjust your counting to match it
5. Play the pattern pizzicato on your instrument

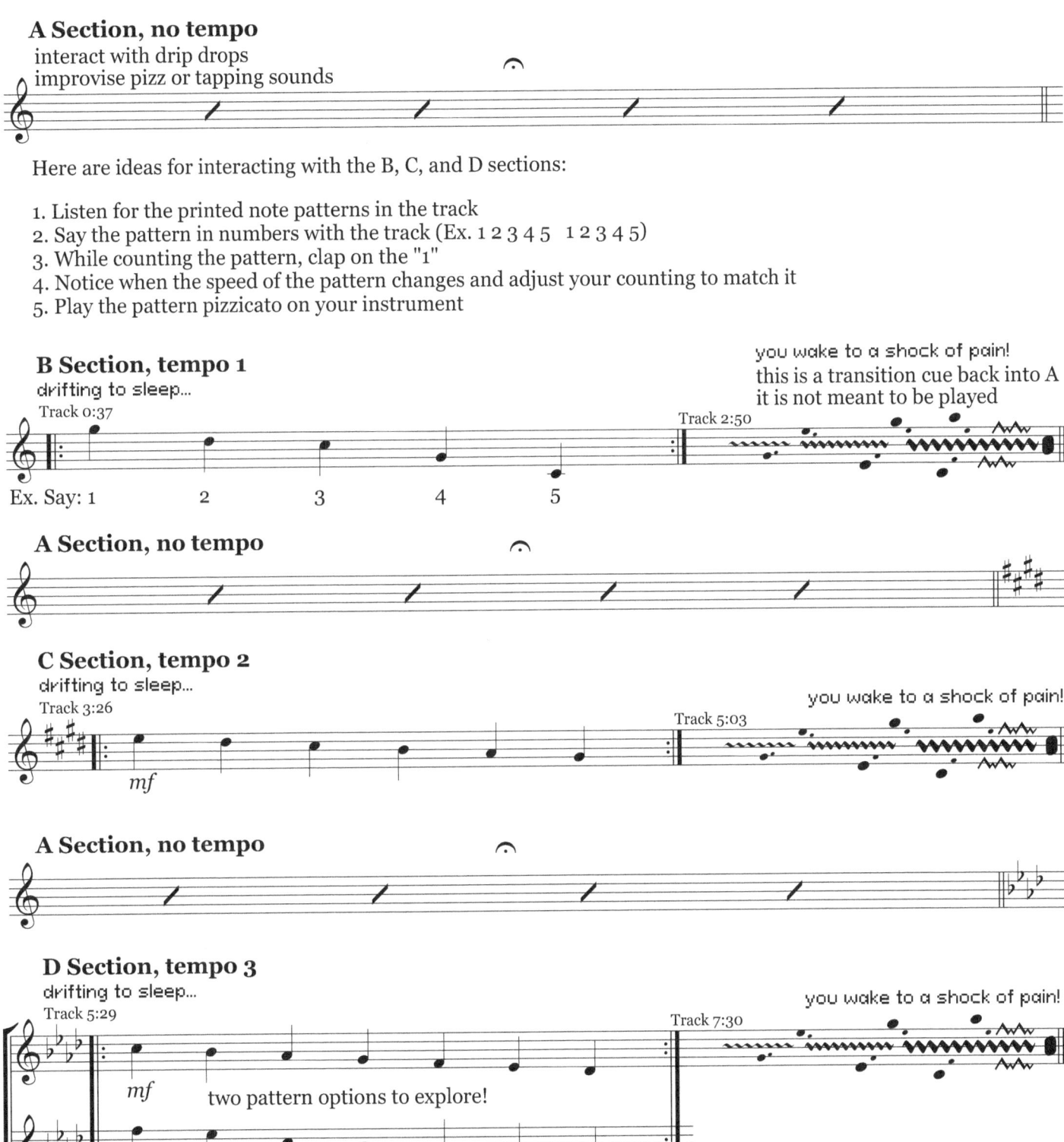

B Section, tempo 1

drifting to sleep...

Track 0:37

you wake to a shock of pain!
this is a transition cue back into A
it is not meant to be played

Track 2:50

Ex. Say: 1   2   3   4   5

A Section, no tempo

C Section, tempo 2

drifting to sleep...

Track 3:26

mf

you wake to a shock of pain!

Track 5:03

A Section, no tempo

D Section, tempo 3

drifting to sleep...

Track 5:29

mf

two pattern options to explore!

you wake to a shock of pain!

Track 7:30

mf

Gravity Dragon

Collapsing with exhaustion and nearly blind from the magi-chemical jolts to your eyes, you feel your heart throb anew with anticipation as you behold the Chronospear gleaming before you, nearly within your grasp. But as you extend your hand to seize it, you recall Arlith's sharp warning: touching the spear is an act that will stir Nythrag, an ancient and formidable dragon bearing the unique and terrifying power of gravity manipulation. When provoked, Nythrag will retaliate by augmenting gravitational density around her, thus pulling adversaries within reach of her merciless attacks. Her deadliest assault, a crushing spike of gravitational energy, devours even the essence of light itself.

The only path to victory: infusing your spirit energy into the Chronospear and using it to manipulate the fabric of time to escape the gravitational forces at play in the present moment. Yet this weapon demands an immense toll on your spirit energy, a dire risk. If Nythrag isn't swiftly vanquished, the insatiable drain could lead to your own demise. With a burning resolve, you gulp down your third potion, grab the Chronospear, and prepare to wage a battle for the very future of humanity.

With a deafening roar, the beast emerges from the depths and surges toward you. Her razor-like obsidian scales scrape the walls, scattering sparks in your direction that illuminate the cavern. The ensuing clash unfolds in a cataclysmic maelstrom that threatens to rend the very heart of the mountain asunder. Nythrag's massive lungs heave out a relentless onslaught of gravity blasts, each of which you somehow evade through the auspices of the Chronospear, haphazardly sending yourself backward and forward in time as you begin to learn the particulars of its use. As the battle intensifies, you perceive a bewildering phenomenon in the air around you as you dodge the beast's attacks—a multitude of your own reflections accumulate in the dank atmosphere of the cavern, a kaleidoscope of afterimages born from your newfound temporal prowess. For a brief moment, disbelief mingles with awe as you grapple with the extraordinary manifestation of your augmented abilities. But fresh attacks from the fearsome gravity dragon pull you back to your primary focus: survival.

15. Nythrag

Nick Revel

Master the Chronospear's temporal abilities while you battle the mighty dragon!

The big bad boss fight has arrived! Can you gather everything you've learned so far to play like a rockstar and slay the dragon?

Victory

After you deliver the final decisive blow to the colossal Nythrag, her gargantuan form crumbles into a seething mass of molten flesh, collapsing with a hiss of fading malevolence. With her dying breath, a sinister proclamation escapes her lips: "Hapless youth, though you have bested me, you will never defeat true evil, for it eternally dwells within the hearts of humanity."

As her venomous words linger in your ears, from the recesses of her decaying chest emerges the Sacred Spirit Crystal, gleaming with an otherworldly radiance. Arlith and Wolf convey their elation through the communication crystal, their jubilant voices echoing in your heart. Setting aside the monster's vicious pronouncement, you join in the exultation of the moment; your triumph, a monumental achievement, calls for a joyful victory dance. But the prospect of raising your limbs in celebration is impossible: your battle with Nythrag has left you so depleted you fear you will not endure the journey back. As you crumple to the cavern floor, you feel the press of a vial in your pocket, the last of Arlith's precious potions. You uncap the vial and drink, overcome with gratitude.

Now you must find a way out of this fetid lair. Searching for an exit, you behold a glimmer of light, scarcely more than a pinprick, emanating from the darkness behind Nythrag's lifeless form. Buoyed by the elation of victory, you follow this faint luminescence. To your delight, you discover a hidden shortcut leading out of the cavern to the base of Mount Wyrmcrest. The call of home pulls you onward, retracing your path through the murky depths of Charnel Marsh and bringing you back to the safety of Raeganthia. Here, you, Arlith, and Wolf share an embrace of celebratory reunion.

16. Victory

Nick Revel

You've earned a glorious respite from challenging battles

This etude has many paths to victory! Can you play the floating note names (C-F-C-G...) in tempo to hear the roots of the chords? Can you play those notes but in the printed rhythms? Can you improvise some rhythms to those notes? As a challenge, can you play the written material?

A Respite From Evil

Soothed by the hard-earned moment of elation and camaraderie, you are basking in the comfort of Arlith's presence when you witness her countenance undergo a sudden transformation, from warm glow to stern determination. You inquire if everything is all right. With a grim sigh, she reveals that by now, Void is undoubtedly aware of your challenges to its gatekeepers, and is likely to exploit this moment of your exhaustion to attack. The only remedy, she declares, is to fortify the dimensional barrier between Void Realm and the physical plane before he can make a move.

"Your body and soul are eager for rest, I know. But before that there is one more thing we must do," she instructs, grasping your hand in hers. "Join me in channeling every possible ounce of spirit energy into the crystal. Together, we shall prevent the immediate return of Void. While you have grown strong and proven yourself worthy of the title of Hero, you are not yet ready to face him. There are further truths you must learn." Weary though you are, the gravity of her words resonates inside you, and you brace yourself for the task at hand.

Hands locked in an unbreakable embrace with Wolf at your side for support, you and Arlith direct your remaining reserves of spirit energy into the Scared Spirit Crystal, thereby fortifying the dimensional barrier that shields the physical realm from Void's wrath. As you feel the energy drain from your body, you sense the presence of unknown others across space and time, willing you to renew the defense they sacrificed their lives for in order to secure the continued safety of humanity.

Nearly collapsing with exhaustion from this massive transfer of energy, you finally sit down with your companions to have a meal. You savor the bounty of the moment in the company of your friends, fellow warriors who seek to defend the world from the certain destruction intended by Void. Not long after, you finally succumb to the embrace of a profoundly restful sleep. But as the sweet echoes of your recent victories reverberate in your dreams, murmurs of fear disturb your peaceful slumber: the nightmarish visage of Void infiltrates your sleep.

"Take comfort, young one," Arlith's calming voice whispers through your fitful agitation. "Tomorrow begins the work to ensure that you have learned all you require before facing Void. But for now, rest."

Chapter Five
Side Quests

Introduction to Side Quests

Side quests are a way to level up your skills to prepare you for more challenging encounters to come. They can be done in any order, sidestepped, and revisited whenever you like.

Troubadour Consort

As you prepare for the final battle with Void, Arlith sends you around the world in search of the very best equipment, artifacts, and ancient texts in order to maximize your chances of victory. Along the way, you refine your skills and endeavor to improve your endurance as well.

During your travels through a remote cliffside kingdom you are mistaken for a rather prominent musician due to your uncanny resemblance. Your protests of ignorance in the ways of music are disregarded; the earl for whom you are expected to perform is adamant that you will tarnish his reputation if you shirk your entertainment duties at an important upcoming ball. While you wonder where the *real* instrumentalist has gotten to, the fact is that you have no time to find them. Though a mage and not a musician yourself, you must join the Troubadour Consort.

You decide it's best to not cause a scene. As magic is virtually unknown in the world beyond a select few practitioners, your only hope is to draw upon your spirit energy to get you through the performance. Luckily Arlith knows a few things about music, and teaches you the basics via the communication crystal. But as you struggle to decipher the notation on the sheet music provided, you notice the real Troubadour's notes describing the previous performance; could they help you somehow?

Unfortunately, your first playthrough with the Consort sounds off. Will you be ready to perform for the earl?

17. Troubadour Consort

A very public performance

Nick Revel

Player Note: This manuscript, a transcription of last ball's performance as I remember it, reflects the earl's demands for higher sonorities

Tema *Originial key and chords. Use as reference*

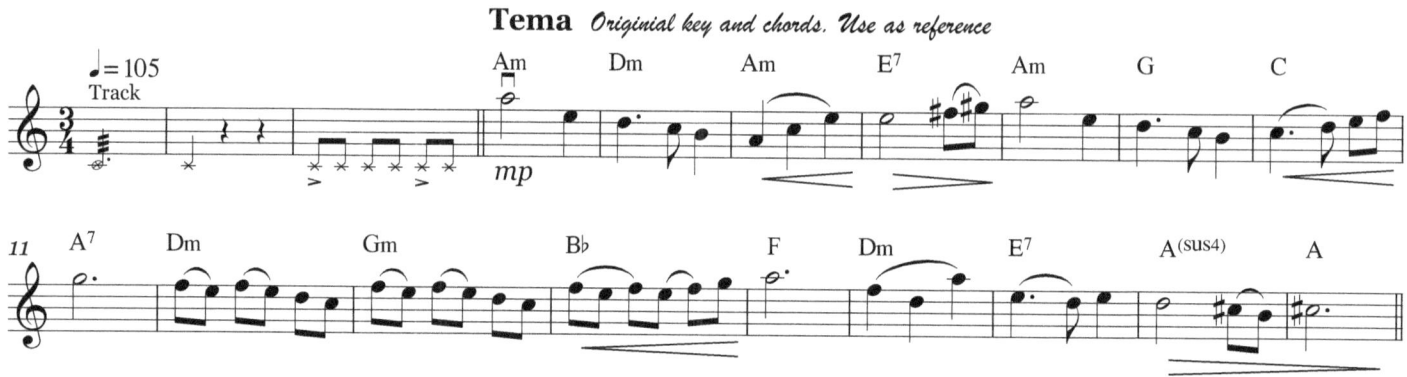

Var. 1 *a normal variation*

Var. 2 *the earl demands we "end lofty"... fool*

Var. 3 *normal variation...thank the Lord*

Var. 4 *the result of the earl's request for a "brighter and more lively" variation...fool...*

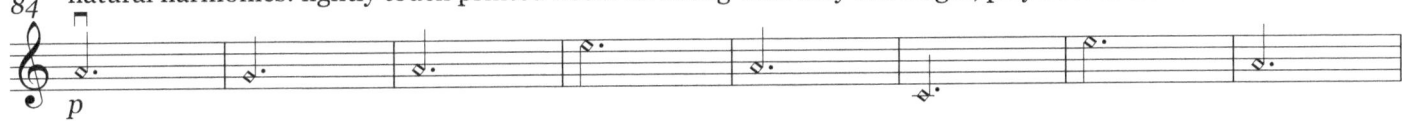

Var. 5 *the result of the earl's request for an even HIGHER variation...fool...*

natural harmonics: lightly touch printed notes on string with only one finger, play bow as normal

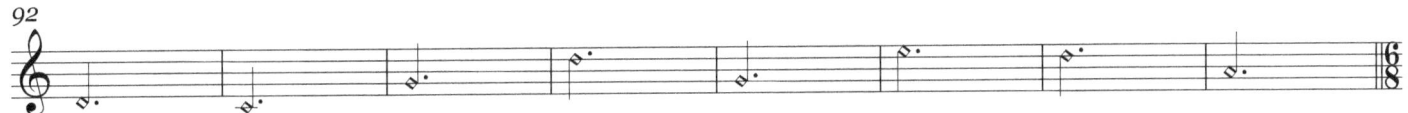

Var. 6 *Page 3 in process. Do remember to collect before performance*

Soundbath

After endless treks, fierce battles, and assuming the crushing responsibility of literally preparing to save humanity, you feel absolutely spent. You hear of a place where weary travelers can rest and renew themselves, a spa with famous baths that are said to have healing properties. Reasoning that you must remain in tip-top condition, you resolve to visit in order to refresh yourself.

After arriving, you make your way in sandals and robe toward the baths and immediately begin to feel the tension melt away. Lowering yourself into the water and closing your eyes, you allow your mind to clear and realize that you sense a vibration in the pool. After a moment or two of puzzlement, you relax with understanding: the natural spirit energy in the bath soothes and refreshes the hearts of weary folk just as much as the warm waters do their bodies.

You let go, allowing the spa's vibrations to wash over you. The soak restores your vitality and reminds you that sometimes, the right choice is to pause for a bit and fill your heart with appreciation for the wonders and beauty around you.

18. Soundbath

Nick Revel

Rest, relax, and restore your energy

This etude acts as a type of meditation. There is no sheet music. To interact with this etude, find the two corresponding audio play-alongs in this chapter's playlist. One is a guided meditation and contains verbal instructions on how to participate, for which you will need your instrument. The other contains only the ambient soundscape, with which you can interact however you like.

Around the World

One of the many towns you pass through houses an orphanage run by a rather eccentric old man named Cid, who in his spare time designs strange and wonderful constructions of metal. His "machines," as he calls them, possess parts that must fit together exactly in order to efficiently transform energy, or "fuel," into mechanical movement. With a shy pride, he demonstrates the simple toys he devises to amuse the children, including one strange and seemingly pointless box with a switch on its top panel that, when flicked, initiates a metal arm. Confusingly, the arm simply emerges from the box and flicks the switch back to the "off" position, then retracts back into the box. "Funny, right?" he exclaims. You scratch your head in puzzlement, but smile nonetheless. In spite of yourself, you are charmed by his outlandish inventions and touched by his evident love for the orphans in his care. Having grown up in an orphanage yourself, you ask if there's anything you can do to help.

With a sigh, he confides that he's in a tough position: out of love for these children, he rashly accepted a bet that seems impossible to win. One of the town's wealthiest (and nastiest) citizens, Sir Faulkman, made Cid a wager: if Cid can build an airship and sail around the world by the end of the season, upon his successful return Faulkman will provide housing, renovations, food, and clothing to the orphanage for the following decade—a lifesaving prospect for an establishment always on the verge of destitution. If Cid fails, however, Faulkman will use his influence to cut all the town's subsidies to the orphanage, thus finally ridding his beautiful town of what he considers undesirables, vagrants, and riffraff. You hear Cid's predicament with alarm, but when a wickedly delightful vision of Faulkman's bitter and seemingly unimaginable defeat flashes through your mind, you vow to help Cid win this impossible bet.

With excitement, you tell Cid about the concept of spirit energy and offer a small demonstration. After a brief fit of ecstatic chattering brought on by this new knowledge, Cid recovers his composure and the two of you dive into creating an airship that runs on spirit energy. The work goes quickly; the genius of Cid's design process is astonishing, and he quickly incorporates the potential of this new energy source. Soon the airship is finished—a modest vessel with just enough room for two people plus supplies, but enough to get the job done, you hope. Because the airship requires a constant output of spirit energy for the machine to convert to thrust, you must accompany Cid on his voyage. With calculated boldness, the two of you spread word through the town about the upcoming event to ensure Faulkman's appearance at the launch.

After a successful takeoff, the voyage proves to be an incredible experience: the sights you share with Cid as you cruise through the air will remain some of your fondest memories as an adventurer. Just as sweet will be the memory of the livid and humiliated Faulkman as you meet the ground upon your return.

19. Around the World

Nick Revel

...in an airship!

Enjoy the view from above as the Hero's theme and its chord progression modulate to a new key every eight bars. Can you follow the pattern to make it all the way around the world? There is no audio play-along for this etude.

Here are some ideas:

1. Play with your friend/teacher. Play the same line, assign top/bottom, or individually decide which line to play.
2. Create your own audio play-along. Record yourself playing one line. Play along with the recording you made.
2. Improvise different rhythmic patterns, arpeggiations, double stops, or counter melodies in the bottom line.
3. Following the harmonic pattern, notate the rest of the progression in the blank staff paper provided.
4. When you grow tired of the chord progression, reharmonize the melody to your liking.

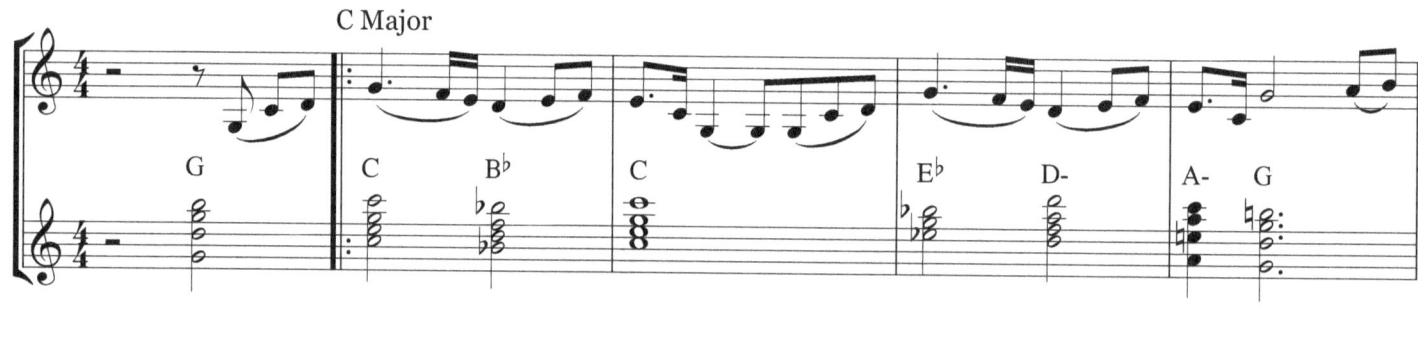

Ancient Scroll

Along your travels through a desolate desert, you encounter ancient ruins unmarked on any map. In the center of the rubble you discover a perfectly preserved door, which leads to a tomb, sealed long ago and undisturbed through time. After breaching it, you begin to explore inside. One item in particular, a visibly ancient scroll, catches your eye as it rests on a weathered stone pedestal. You touch it warily, but to your surprise, no monsters descend from the ceiling, no blades or points explode out of the walls, and no poison mist fills the air. The significance of this situation eludes you. What document would be afforded this place of importance, yet remain unprotected by traps? What secrets might be held within the ancient wisdom of this scroll?

Opening it with care, you endeavor to decipher it, but find no sense in its logic or meaning. Your attempts to interpret its motifs range from literal—trying to sound out the symbols on the page as an onomatopoeia—to abstract—making whatever sounds or incantations come to you spontaneously. After each attempt, you wait and see if a spell has been cast that has changed your environment or yourself, but nothing special happens. Perhaps there is no wisdom here; maybe it was just some ancient's to-do list. But then, why the pedestal? Your curiosity keeps you coming back again and again. Maybe one day, you will crack the mystical code.

20. Ancient Scroll
What does it mean???

Nick Revel

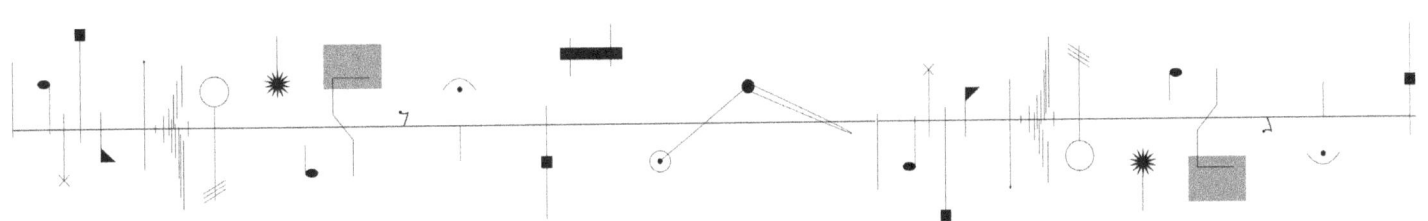

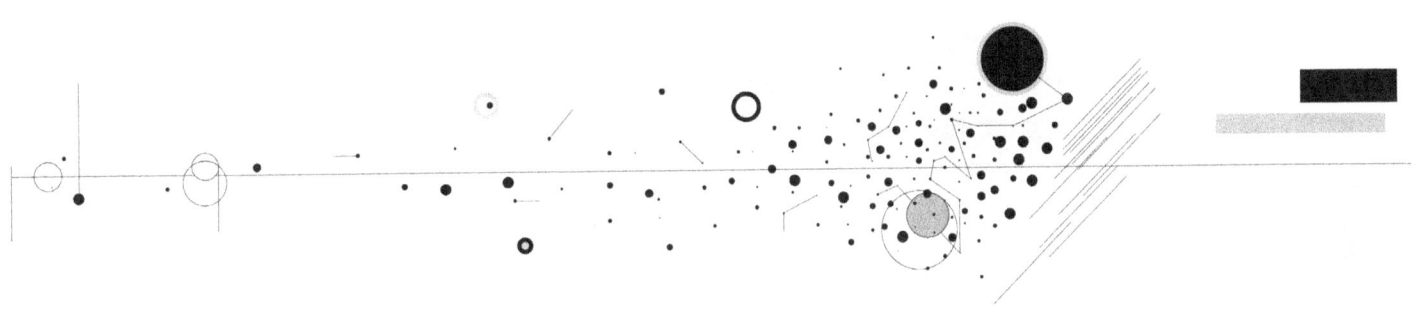

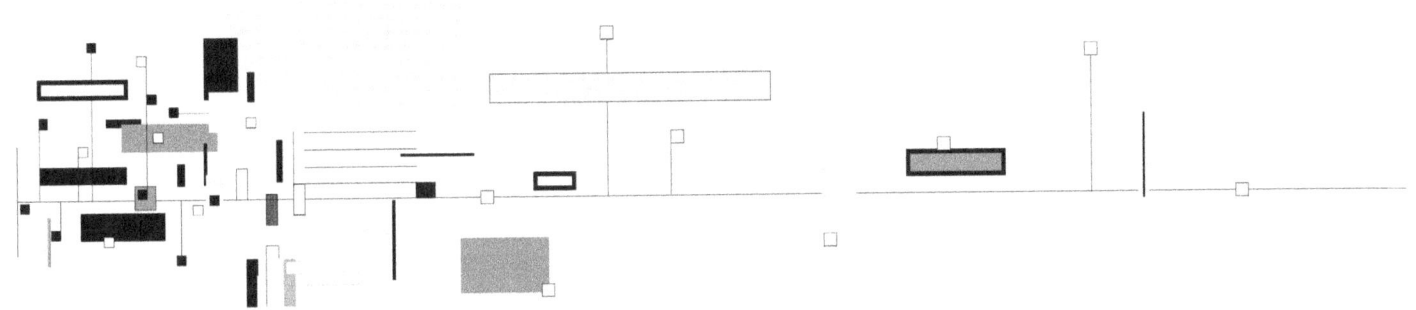

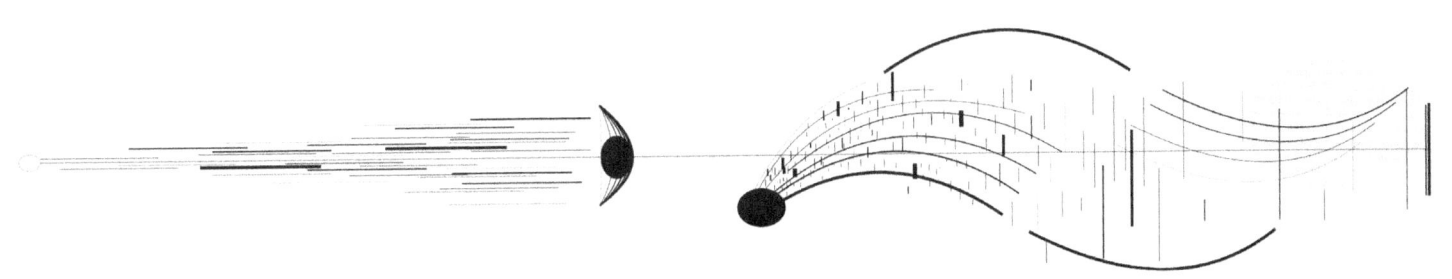

Dance Battle

Your defeat of the mighty Nythrag in the Obsidian Caverns before your return to Raeganthia and subsequent side quests has given you well-earned confidence in your abilities. However, in the course of your quest to find the ultimate items to vanquish Void, perhaps you've grown a bit *over*confident.

After venturing boldly into one particularly exotic dungeon—carved from solid granite, adorned with gothic spires and statues of what appear to be demons of a past world—you are greeted by what can only be described as a vampire. Yet in spite of his long gaunt face, slicked-back black hair, and immaculate collared cloak he seems intelligent, civilized, and curiously lacking a demon's typical bloodlust.

"Good evening, young adventurer," he intones with an unplaceable accent. "My name is Count Funkula. Welcome to my humble abode." With a sinister smirk and an inviting wave of his cape, he offers you a deal: "Fight me... in the ultimate dance battle! If you win, you survive. If you lose, you die!" He cackles devilishly and you hear the dungeon gates slam shut behind you. Escape is impossible. You must dance like your life depends on it!

What a predicament you've gotten yourself into! But there is no time to think. All around you, colorful rays of light begin flashing in sync with a complex array of vibrations coursing through the air; some kind of music, perhaps, but in an arrangement of patterns and tones you've never heard before. All of a sudden, you find yourself being manipulated like a puppet, your limbs forced into rhythmic gyrations in sync with his strange music, at the cost of your own precious physical energy! Caught off guard by the sensory overload, you struggle to focus. Directing your gaze toward the vampire, you observe thin strands of spirit energy emanating from each of the fingers on his outstretched hands, which have attached themselves to your limbs. To your horror, you grasp the grim end game: should you fail to exert your own spirit energy to defy Funkula's control of your body, you will succumb to lethal exhaustion. Thinking fast, you realize you must turn the tables on Funkula. You send out and attach your own strands of spirit energy to his limbs, thus closing the loop and directing the same taxing choreography dictated by the vampire back at him. Now *he* must move in time with *your* dance! Your gazes locked in perfect synchronicity, the ultimate dance battle has begun.

By the end, both of you wield each other's bodies with impeccably timed spirit energy, as if in a highly rehearsed choreography. When the cavern's echo of the last note faded to silence, you both collapse to the ground, legs and arms burning with fatigue, able to only pant heavily and look across at each other. You are almost too tired to wonder what will happen next. But to your surprise, Funkula starts to laugh from the bottom of his belly. "Young adventurer, I have not had so much fun in a millennium! You are the first to be able to keep pace with me. Thank you for this experience. You have reminded me what it means to be alive." Reeling from the insane depravity of this demon, who values his own entertainment over the lives of others, you hear the massive gates groan open once more and decide it's best to leave before more chaos ensues. "Come visit any time!" you hear Funkula call weakly after you with a chuckle. "I've got great snacks!"

21. Dance Battle

Can you out-funk Count Funkula himself?

Nick Revel

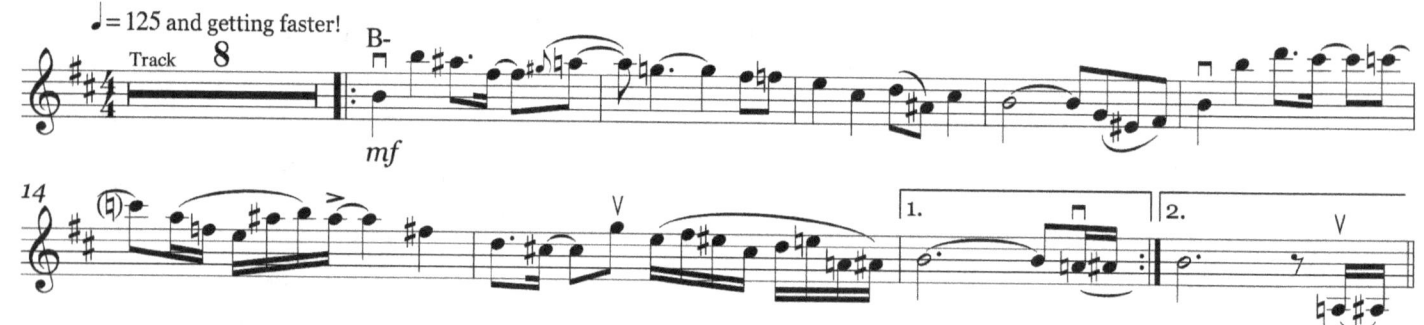

Unlock this level in
LEGEND
difficulty

The Truth Beckons

With each passing adventure, you have gained experience, confidence, and humility, thus solidifying your status as a full-fledged world-class adventurer. Despite allowing yourself much-needed moments of joy and contentment during your recent travels, the underlying threat of Void has remained ever present, just beyond view.

As you contemplate the next step in your journey, Arlith's presence suddenly beams into your consciousness through the communication crystal, urgently summoning you back to Anchorstone. Her cryptic message hints at something concerning the Sacred Crystal. Having learned from experience that Arlith's mysterious messages precede world-shattering revelations, you gird yourself to face the unknown that lies ahead.

Chapter Six

End Game

God Realm

Arlith has recalled you from your adventuring for a very important reason.

"The time has come for us to prepare to make our move against Void," she declares. "Before all else, you must acquaint yourself thoroughly with the Sacred Spirit Crystal. It is vital to your quest, and your spirit energy must be able to merge with it seamlessly if you are to use it to its full capacity."

As you prepare for this solemn undertaking, Arlith advises you to touch the crystal only once you are completely ready. When you ask how you will know, Arlith smiles, enigmatic and amused at the same time. "You will *know*," she promises, leaving you to your meditation.

You sit alone before the inert crystal. With your eyes closed, you try to calm your mind, breathing slowly and deeply to relax your body. Time passes. You have no idea how long you sit there before something tugs at the edge of your consciousness.

Voices call out to you, repeating your name and inviting you to touch the crystal. You open your eyes and your gaze falls upon the pale blue radiance now emanating from the sacred gem. Without hesitation, your fingers reach out to make contact with the precious stone.

The instant your skin meets the crystal's surface, an unexpected sensation envelops you. With an infusion of ethereal energy that courses through your being, your surroundings blur and shift, replaced by a brilliant expanse that leaves you bewildered and disoriented.

You are on a different plane. Here, an abundance of light seems to cascade from all directions. The air itself is dense with a gossamer-white mist, clouding your vision. Pillowy golden clouds drift in the distance, emanating a strange yet captivating grandeur.

The voices calling to you gradually grow clearer, and you become aware of the presence of three distinct figures. The first to reveal himself is Cael, his welcoming smile radiating warmth. "Hello, Hero," he greets you gently. "Welcome to God Realm. Your journey has led you here, and your arrival is a testament to your strength. I foresaw your path from the moment you set foot in Eldervale. Please know that I bear no ill will toward you. The battle we waged was a test of your spirit, a test you passed admirably. I was eager to escape the wretched form that Void had imposed upon me, and your victory saved me. I am content and at peace now.

"Here in God Realm," he explains, "only those with the purest spirits are able to conserve their consciousness and identity after crossing over. Those with less pure essence simply return to divine aether. Having thankfully retained my consciousness here," he continues, "I have been eager to meet you on this plane."

He looks at you sympathetically. "But beholding the essence of divinity is an overwhelming experience for a human, is it not? You must be suffering an immense strain from the weight and density of spirit energy in this place. We have a purpose in bringing you here, however. Our intention is to give you crucial information to fulfill your purpose... and there are those who eagerly await a reunion with you," he adds with a quiet smile. "I will depart for now, but I shall send you all my strength when you confront Void. Remember, Hero," he says, enveloping you in radiant warmth, "you are strong! When you return to the realm of humans, please give my love to Arlith and Wolf. For now, I bid you farewell."

As Cael's form disperses into the vapor, two new figures coalesce before you, their voices resonating in unison. "Dear one," they greet you warmly. "It has been our greatest joy to watch you blossom into a remarkable, wise, courageous, intelligent, and kind human. Meeting you here again after all these years transcends words. We've missed you so much, and we have much to share with you. We are your parents, Lilia and Eonan. Leaving you with Rowena in Amberglade while we marched to almost certain death was the most difficult decision of our lives. Our hearts burned with grief every step of the way. While we understand that your feelings toward us may be complicated, and harbor no expectation of forgiveness, we hope you will allow us to teach you the mastery of the Sacred Spirit Crystal. First, you must gain a deeper understanding of Void.

"In his former life," they continue, "Void was a human named Nuba, cursed with unusual and frightening black eyes that made him a pariah. Shortly after his seventh birthday, a plague descended upon his village, claiming lives and causing crop failures. The villagers, their suffering unbearable, held Nuba responsible. They expelled his family from the village into the wilderness, only for Nuba's parents to push him into the river and return to their home. Astonishingly, Nuba survived, but paid for his continued existence with an enduring hatred and distrust for humanity. As a result, his spirit energy turned black, and, after a life of great suffering, in death he sealed himself into what he then named Void Realm, maintaining his consciousness due to the dark purity of his spirit energy.

"Your spirit energy," Lilia and Eonan continue, "is a stark contrast to Void's rage. Your spirit embodies compassion, even in the face of adversity. *You* extend second chances to those who have erred, while Void hungers for vengeance, seeking the utter annihilation of humanity using his own Dark Spirit Crystal.

"Yet it isn't as simple as pure good versus evil. Every person is born to this world with both light and dark spirit energies within them. When we confronted Void years ago in the Eldervale Wilds, we were unprepared to face our own shadows when he drew them to the forefront of our spirits. Those nagging doubts and insecurities—of ourselves and humanity—drained our strength within the Void Realm. As Void's dark spirit energy seeped from the Sacred Spirit Crystal into the surrounding environment through the dimensional breach, triggering the demonification of nearby forest creatures, Wolf valiantly defended our vulnerable physical forms from their attacks.

Desperate to save us, Cael withdrew our spirits from that desolate place and returned us to our bodies, but it was too late: Void had depleted us irrevocably. In our final moments, we recognized the extent of our sacrifice—a life with you—and passed you what remained of our spirit energy, seeking to make amends for our actions. Cael and Arlith channeled their own remaining energy into fortifying the weakened dimensional barrier, a temporary measure that sealed away Void Realm.

"Learn from our experience," they implore you. "Your confrontation with Void must be unwavering resolute, devoid of doubt. But fear not: when the time comes, we will guide you in the use of the Sacred Spirit Crystal to traverse to Void Realm. Please persevere, and know our hearts travel with you. We are immensely proud of you, and we love you completely. You are our most profound achievement."

22. God Realm

Nick Revel

Struggling to withstand the intense pressure of massive spiritual energy

This etude is an introduction to shifting! Since each line is an 8-bar phrase and uses the
same chord progression, you can play as written or repeat the same line.

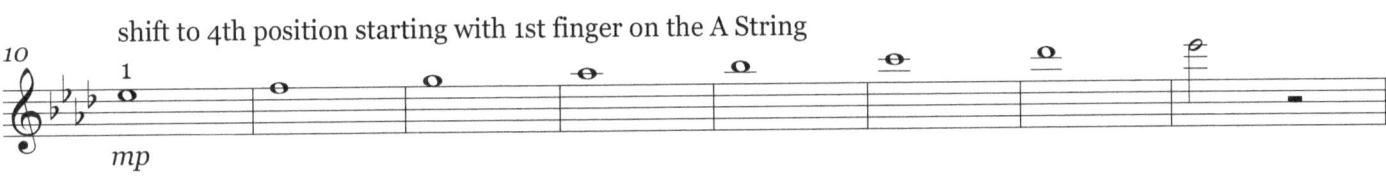

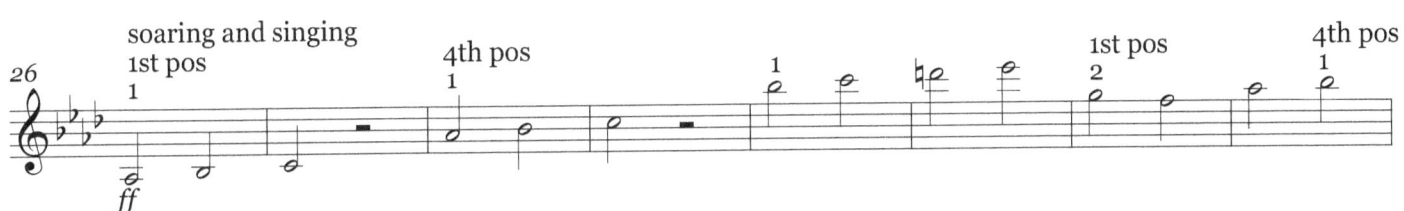

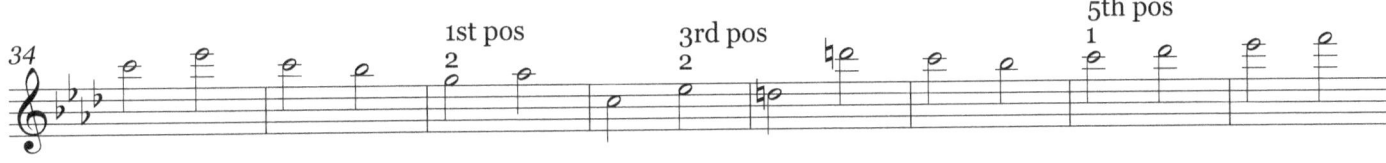

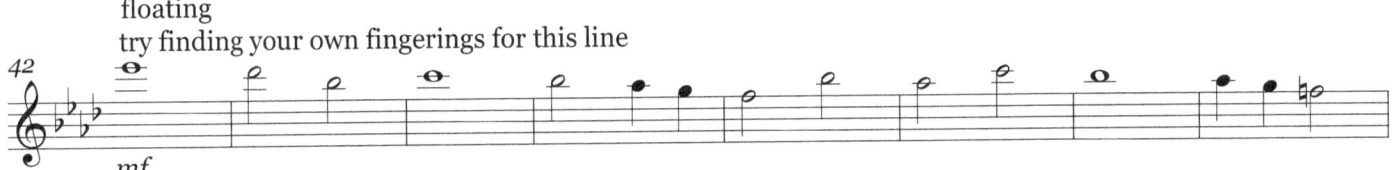

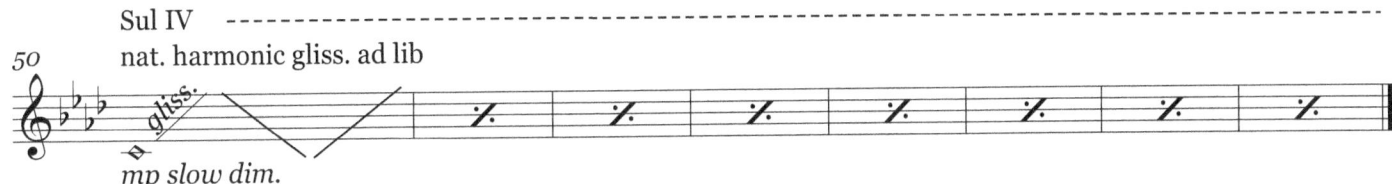

The Hero Returns

This encounter, the most energetically and emotionally intense experience of your entire life, leaves you momentarily disoriented. Blinking in astonishment, you look around to see that you are no longer in God Realm: you stand before none other than the familiar gates of Amberglade—your home. Your parents and Cael, you now realize, have orchestrated your return, a gift before your final confrontation with Void. A flood of emotions surges within you. The overwhelming knowledge about Void and the Sacred Spirit Crystal, Cael's profound forgiveness for the violence you inflicted upon him, and the momentous encounter with your long lost parents leave you grappling for understanding.

However, there's no time for contemplation. Just down the road, you see Aunt Rowena sweeping leaves. She looks up, and upon seeing you, she drops her rake to the ground and sprints towards you as fast as her elderly body allows. Her tears and fervent embrace are a testament to the agony she, along with the entire orphanage, endured in your absence. They believed you lost in the cavern's collapse in Eldervale, she says, the protagonist in a tragic tale of a bright young adventurer felled in their first encounter with adversity. How wonderful to know they'd been wrong.

News of your return spreads like wildfire throughout Amberglade, and soon a crowd gathers. You move through heartwarming chaos, embracing each familiar figure who mourned your departure and yearned for your unlikely return. Your remarkable deeds not only earn the respect of your fellow villagers, but also kindle a profound sense of kinship and unity.

The tender warmth that envelops you during this jubilant reunion slowly transforms into a bittersweet nostalgia. As the joyful encounters continue and then settle, you're acutely aware that, much as your parents did years ago, you must pass once more out of the town gates and tread an unknown and sobering path. Beyond them, the ominous specter of Void, harbinger of destruction, awaits your call to destiny.

23. The Hero Returns

A bittersweet reunion

Nick Revel

You've made it back home! But you feel sad because your mission is not yet complete and you must leave once again.
Can you bring out these emotions in this etude? Sing the top line while your teacher or friend plays the bottom line.

Cantabile con molto rubato

Breaching Void Realm

Deep in the Eldervale Wilds, you, Arlith, and Wolf gather to make final preparations for your impending spirit warp from this plane to the dimension of Void's realm. In the center of your circle rests the Sacred Spirit Crystal, its presence pulsating with an otherworldly energy. From God Realm, the ethereal voices of Cael and your parents guide you through the intricate steps required to activate the crystal in order to propel your consciousness into the ominous Void Realm. You grasp the stark implications of this procedure: your spirit energy and consciousness alone will travel into this dimension, leaving behind your vulnerable corporeal form under the protection of Wolf, who will battle the forest creatures transformed into giant raging beasts by Void's dark spirit energy.

Cael and your parents continue their guidance, their faint whispers passing through the dimensional barrier, recounting the critical instructions. As preparations conclude, you cannot help but recall that the previous attempt to destroy Void was met with failure. Doubts multiply, and your mind races uncontrollably despite the reassurances from those around you.

Then, amidst your mental and emotional turmoil, your parents declare that the moment has arrived. Wolf, wearing the precious Talaria and armed with the Blur Stone and Chronospear, steps forward, a guttural snarl erupting from her throat. Her bloodlust is evident; she is more than ready for the impending onslaught of beasts brought forth from dark spirit energy that will seep through the Sacred Spirit Crystal during your battle with Void.

With a shared grip on the crystal, you and Arlith initiate the spirit warp. A torrent of energy surges through you, reminiscent of your previous sojourn in God Realm. Blinking blindly in this new sea of darkness, illuminated solely by sporadic pockets of low-density spirit energy, you try to move, but the very atmosphere resists your efforts. A gravity that seems twice as potent as usual hinders your progress, leaving you feeling sluggish and graceless. In spite of these daunting circumstances, you muster your resolve, propelling yourself forward into the abyss, bound for an inevitable confrontation with Void.

24. Void Realm

The way forward is uncertain

Nick Revel

You're lost in the crush of the Void! Explore playing doublestops. Play them in any order.
There is no meter or tempo, so decide when to play them and for how long. Play with different dynamics
and articulations. Listen for how the double stops interact with the harmonies of the Audio Play-Along.
Section 1: Play in first postion. The lower note is always an open string.
The key signature throughout is 3 flats.

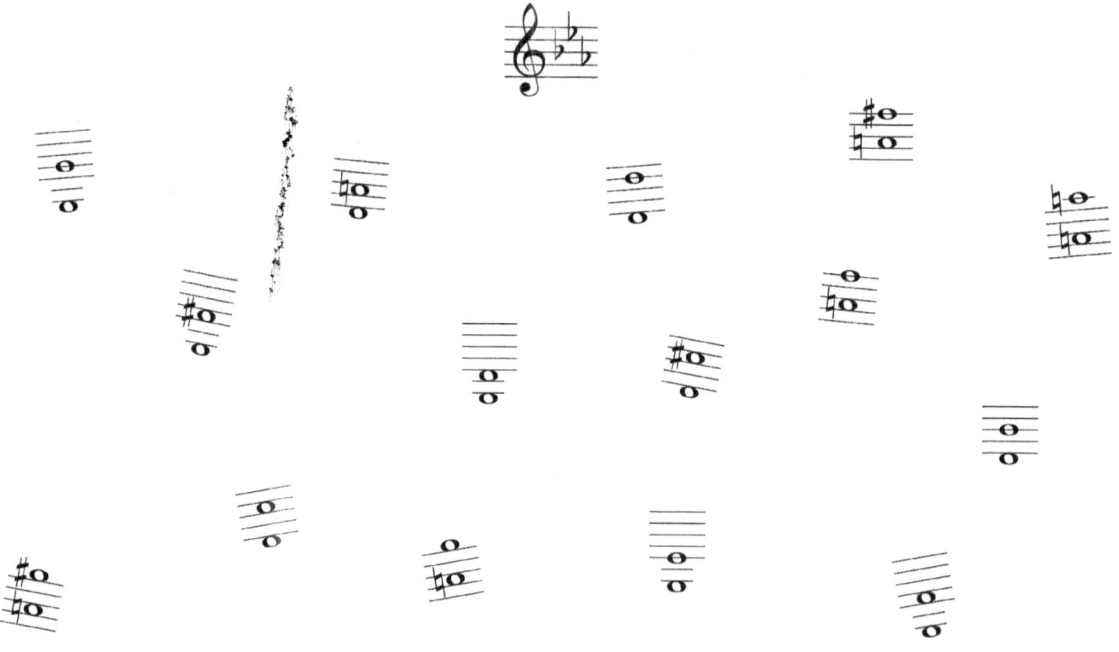

At 3:00, you hear what sounds like an explosion, which you are certain comes from where Void waits

Section 2: Play like above.
Use your higher positions to reach these doublestops. The lower note is always an open string.

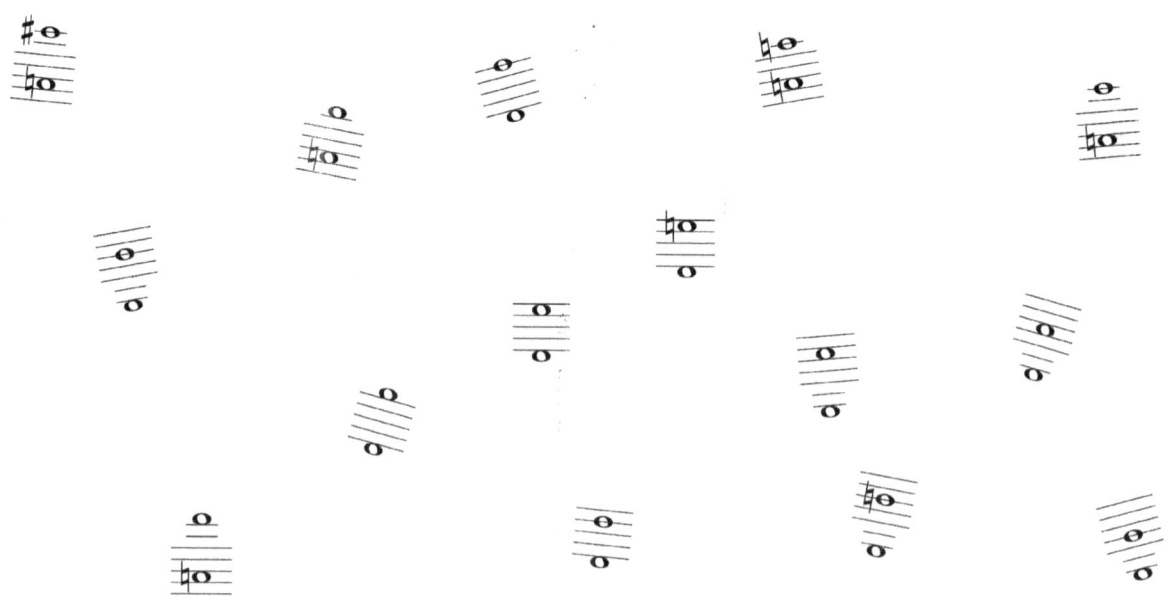

At 6:00 minutes, you hear what sounds like another explosion. You follow the sound.

Section 3: Use at least one open string in each doublestop.

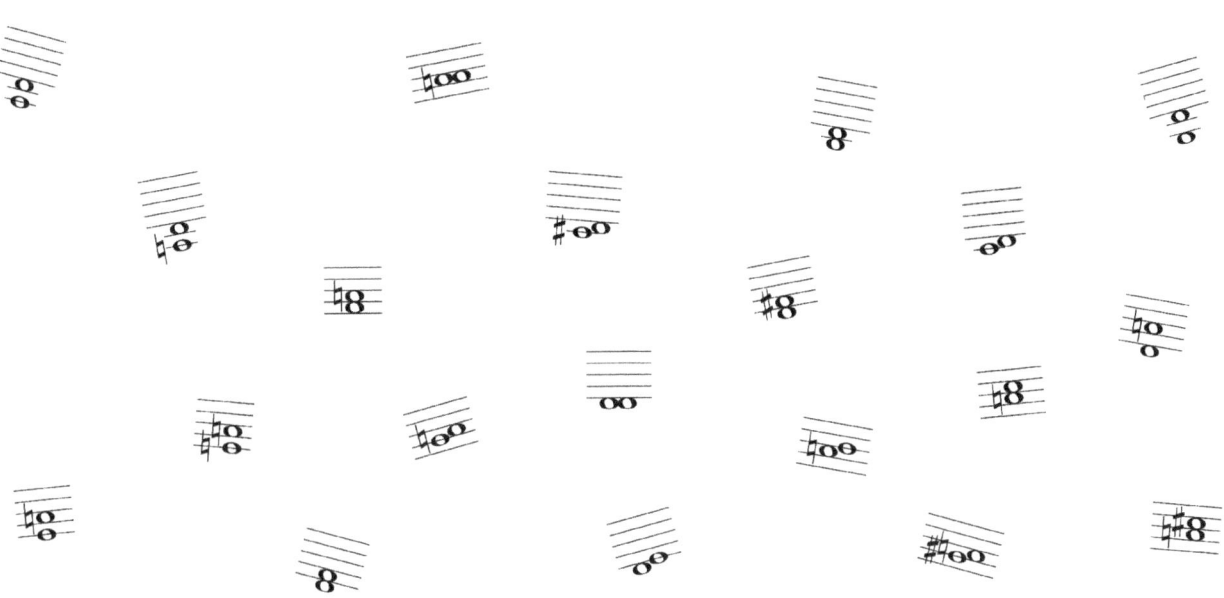

After another explosion at 8:00, the path becomes clearer. Your pace increases as you feel yourself getting closer to Void.

Section 4: Use only one finger to play both notes in each doublestop.

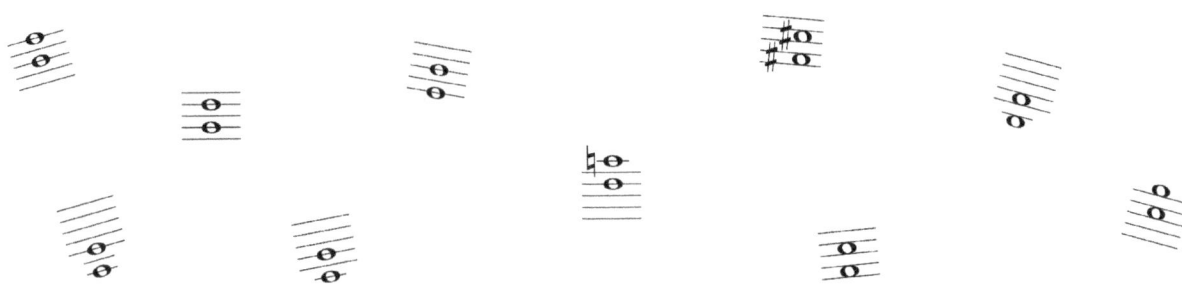

After yet another explosion at 9:30, you see your final destination, where Void waits, and you shift to a near sprint (accelerando). You have 40 seconds until the last explosion.

Section 5: Use different fingers for every note in each doublestop.

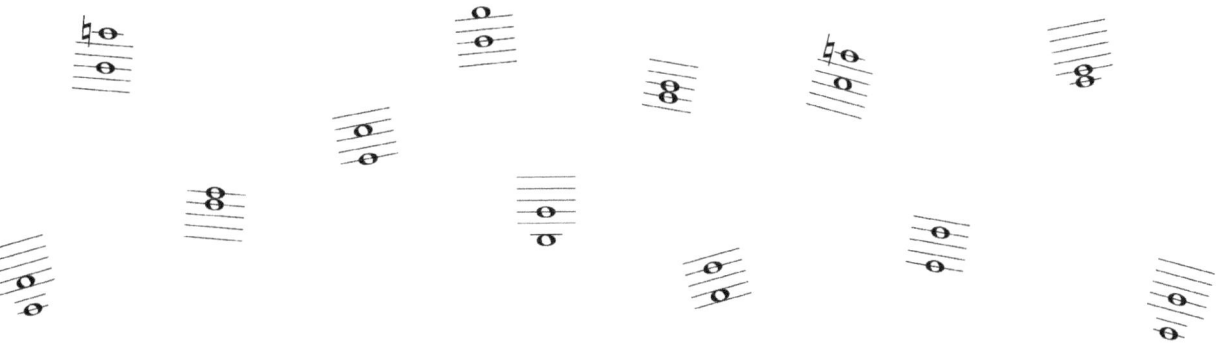

The Fight for Humanity

As you near the core of this desolate dimension, Void's presence emerges like a malevolent specter, a grotesque fusion of rage and delight, relishing in the impending annihilation of your spirit. In response, a sudden surge of fury courses through your being, fueled by memories of the vile curse he laid upon Cael and his hand in the death of your parents. With this anger your thoughts begin to divert from your goal, overflowing into bitterness and resentment as you grieve the life that could have been, growing up with your long-lost parents.

Your resolve falters as you continue to struggle against the relentless atmospheric pressure of Void Realm. The danger of your spirit succumbing to Void's corruptive influence increases, fueled by the welling hatred within you. However, in this dire moment, a lifeline finds its way to you, a thread of your parents' energy trickling gently into your awareness. You sense their embrace.

Arlith's voice comes to you through the communication crystal. "Be strong," she whispers. "Your parents believe in you with all their hearts, but I can channel only this much of their energy to you." Though it is a mere trickle, it revitalizes your spirit, imbuing you with strength, love, and clarity. Your resolve is renewed.

Locked in a fierce gaze with the raging Void, you glimpse the lonely, dark eyes of Nuba looking out at you beneath the seething fury and the buried grief. It dawns upon you, clear as crystal, that the cycle of destruction can only be shattered through forgiveness. With an overwhelming surge of compassion and a resounding cry, you call out to Void directly, using his former name, and offering him your understanding. All of his suffering and the dark path his spirit energy has traversed, you empathize, was the result of circumstances beyond his control. In spite of all of the pain he has caused you, you offer your forgiveness.

In response to your revelation, Void recoils in a cacophonous fit of rage, vehemently rejecting your proffered peace, his eyes ablaze with indignation. He hurls himself forward into an assault, summoning lethal black whips of energy that lash out indiscriminately, a deadly onslaught devoid of a discernible and avoidable pattern. Your senses sharpen, and you become a blur of motion, nimble in your evasive maneuvers, seeking the opportune moment to retaliate. Your compassion gives way to a crystalline understanding: Void must be vanquished, not out of vengeance, but in profound benevolence to the memory of Nuba. By destroying Void, you will relieve his suffering. This clarity fuels your relentless battle, a tempestuous clash of spirits and wills to free the good trapped within an eternity of suffering and destruction.

25. Final Battle
The fight to save humanity

Nick Revel

It all comes down to this! Gather your strength and patience as you attempt to master this etude. Can you learn how this part fits into the Audio Play-Along? Can you learn how to count these challenging meters? Can you come up with fingerings and bowings that make playing the notes and rhythms easier? Use the Audio Play-Along "for VIOLA/CELLO Players" for this Violin Story Mode etude.

stomp (with track snare)
feel 2 equally spaced notes per bar

tremolo

harsh biting staccato pont wild sound

Peace at Long Last

When Void's menacing presence abruptly disintegrates in a cataclysmic explosion, you are overwhelmed by disorientation. As the darkness of the Void Realm dissipates, you catch a fleeting glimpse of a young boy wearing a faint, tired smile, his energy vibrating with gratitude as he fades from view. You feel a rushing sensation, and with a blink you find yourself once again in the forest, sitting opposite Arlith. Her brow is furrowed in profound exertion, beads of sweat glisten on her skin, and crimson trails streak from her nose, eyes, and ears—a testament to the immense strain of communicating spirit energy between Void Realm and the physical plane. She musters a feeble smile before surrendering to exhaustion, mumbling softly as she folds gracefully to the ground, sleep claiming her.

A triumphant growl draws your attention. A few feet to your right, Wolf stands amid a field of corpses. As you battled Void in a different dimension, she protected Arlith and your fragile human body from the attacks of creatures demonified by the darkness of Void Realm leaking through the crack between the worlds. Her colossal frame quivers with exhaustion, splattered with streaks of multi-hued blood. With great effort, she offers you a strained thumbs-up before also collapsing with fatigue.

Through the communication crystal, the ethereal voices of Cael and your parents resonate from God Realm, ringing out in jubilation. Even without Arlith to help facilitate their communication, you can hear them, so strong is their joy. They proclaim your victory, praising your heroism in liberating humanity from the clutches of hatred and through your conquest of Void's malevolence. Overwhelmed with emotion, tears of elation and exhaustion stream down your face.

Your heart brimming with emotion, you turn to the sleeping forms of Arlith and Wolf and fall to your knees in gratitude for their unwavering guidance, wisdom, and protective devotion. Your tears flow as you are overcome with love for Cael and your parents, who willingly gave every iota of their spirit energy to enable this victory. Soon, you can sense, they will dissolve into the boundless aether, harmonizing the equilibrium of light and dark energy in the cosmos. Your time with them has been so short. And yet, in spite of your grief, you feel certain that your spirits will reunite when your time comes to pass out of the physical realm.

Exhausted but at peace, you recline upon the ground alongside Arlith and Wolf, reflecting on the peril that nearly befell the world—an impending catastrophe all but unknown to its inhabitants. For villages, towns, and cities across the great expanse of this world, tomorrow will unfold, a day like any other. But though the world may not have changed, you have changed greatly. You are a Hero, and pledge to carry this hard-won humility, empathy, and forgiveness throughout your journey forward, in this realm and all the others that may await you.

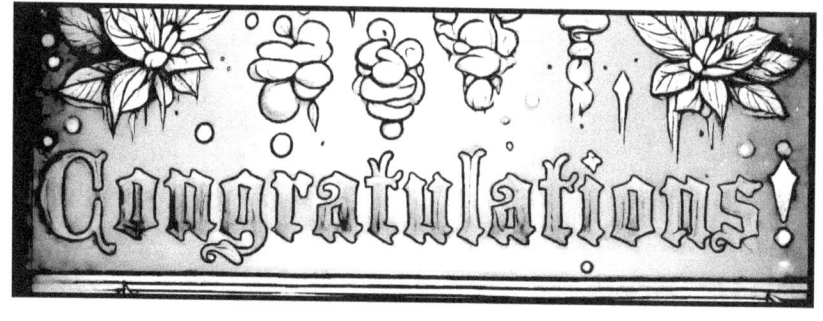

The world is safe at long last...

Thanks to YOU,

and...

Aunt Rowena

Cael Mosshorn

Arlith Rose

Wolf

Your Parents

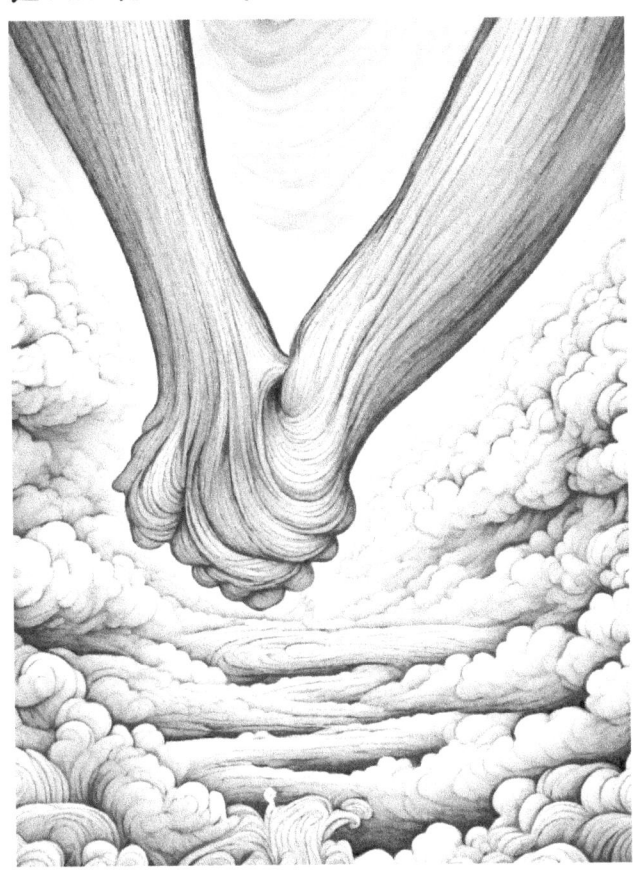

the earl...fool...

Cid

Count Funkula